Grounding Leadership Ethics in African Diaspora and Election Rights

Grounding Leadership Ethics in African Diaspora and Election Rights

Jean-Pierre K. Bongila

LEXINGTON BOOKS
Lanham • Boulder • New York • Toronto • Plymouth, UK

Published by Lexington Books
A wholly owned subsidiary of Rowman & Littlefield
4501 Forbes Boulevard, Suite 200, Lanham, Maryland 20706
www.rowman.com

10 Thornbury Road, Plymouth PL6 7PP, United Kingdom

British Library Cataloguing in Publication Information Available

Library of Congress Cataloging-in-Publication Data

Bongila, Jean-Pierre K., 1961-author.
Grounding leadership ethics in African diaspora and election rights / Jean-Pierre K. Bongila.
pages cm
Includes bibliographical references and index.
ISBN 978-0-7391-6739-7 (cloth : alk. paper) -- ISBN 978-0-7391-6740-3 (electronic)
1. Aesthetics. 2. Postmodernism. I. Rundell, John F. II. Title.
JQ3529.A5B66 2013
324.6'208691096--dc23
2013025865

♾™ The paper used in this publication meets the minimum requirements of American
National Standard for Information Sciences Permanence of Paper for Printed Library
Materials, ANSI/NISO Z39.48-1992.

Printed in the United States of America

To the memory of Mother Marie-Magdeleine Milang Mbutu.
To all practitioners of ethical leadership, particularly Dr. Bruce Kramer.
To the African Diaspora and its leadership.

Contents

Preface

Today's leaders find themselves always confronted with intricate dilemmas of ethical nature that need resolution particularly at the professional, national and global level. I have become increasingly interested in ways aspiring global leaders or those who see themselves as such process their coming to term with serious issues that are not just routine problems one deals with. Of most importance has been my preoccupation with how ethical leaders-to-be, including our own master's and doctorate students at the University of St. Thomas, can empower their followers and colleagues and set the fundamentals for ethical courses of action. Before daring to propose some model or guidelines to such leaders, it was imperative that I get rooted in the discipline of leadership ethics, of which I only had theoretical knowledge as a consequence of my academic formation. Providentially, the teaching of a course for MA, Ed.S, and Ed.D students on "The Intellectual and Ethical Foundations of Leadership" provided me with the impetus I needed to widen my curiosity in this area. As I reshuffled the course syllabus after its first offering, I stumbled upon the DIRR (Description, Interpretation, Rehearsal, and Re-discernment) method of ethical decision making, which Enomoto and Kramer (2007) developed in their book *Leading through the Quagmire*. Little did I know that this book was cowritten by Bruce Kramer, then the department chair of Leadership, Policy, and Administration, and later associate dean for the College of Applied Professional Studies (CAPS). He moved on to become the dean of the CAPS, which has changed since to become the College of Education, Leadership, and Counseling (CELC), and continued to teach "Ethics," a course he has held for doctoral students in leadership for over a decade at the University of St. Thomas, MN.

DIRR might have been one of the puzzles I have been looking for to satisfy my own quest to tackle tough ethical questions at the global level, and provide similar leaders with a tool for dilemma resolution. This method mastered and coupled with "prudent pragmatism" in its final stage was getting much clearer as I communicated it to students and required them to build relating class assignments upon it. In addition, my directing of the International Leadership program and teaching of courses like "International Development," "Leadership in International Contexts," "Development, Underdevelopment, and Education" opens my academic mind to multifaceted ethical dilemmas pertaining to the rapports between the Global South and the Global North. When it comes to world issues, the British Broadcasting Corporation (BBC) is known for lending reliable up-to-date news and information. Sure enough, my reading of the BBC led me to a survey it addressed to the African Diaspora worldwide. The uncharacteristic question read: "With millions of Africans living outside the continent, should more countries give their expats the vote? Or when you leave your country, do you also leave behind your right to have a say in how the country is run? What impact would the diaspora have in your country's politics?"

Armed with ethical leadership theories, familiarized with the DIRR method, and passionate about international issues, the BBC case gave me a first dilemma worth its name that I could use as a sample of ethical analysis and decision making. The fifty-third annual Conference of the African Studies Association in San Francisco, CA offered the most suitable academic arena to lay out my ethical analysis of the dilemma. Questions and comments I received from the highly academic audience indicated interest in the topic as it enhanced my resolve to pursue further research in that direction. As Providence had it, Lexington Books generously offered that I consider publishing a book with them.

In essence the purpose of this book is twofold: first, it makes the point that leadership ethics can bring a special and overdue contribution to the analysis of global issues; second it applies the Description, Interpretation, Rehearsal, and Re-discernment (DIRR) model of ethical decision making proposed by Enomoto and Kramer to a dilemma of global proportion, understanding "whether or not people of African origins who are residing overseas should be granted the rights to vote in their home country elections." A first quick response to the question might be "Why not? They are still citizens of their countries and are constitutionally entitled to vote." Whereas another impulsive answer would say: "No, they cannot vote in their home countries because they do not live in there any longer and do not pay taxes." If some readers find themselves in either side of the dilemma, they would not be alone. Neither African Diaspora themselves nor their homelands are unanimous on this matter. The IDEA (International Institute for Democracy and Electoral Assistance) and the Administration and Cost of Elections (ACE) have revealed that only twenty-eight countries in Africa have a provision for expatriate votes. Of the twenty-eight, only a dozen have actually implemented overseas franchise, with some countries going back and forth between implementation and prohibition of those elections. To make the matter even more intricate, some members of the Diaspora who hold multiple citizenships also request the right to vote in homelands while participating in the suffrage of their country of residence. There is an obvious question of loyalty to any of the countries whose nationality they bear. As frustrating as these discrepancies might appear, they make the point on the challenge posed by a serious ethical dilemma as opposed to "mere problems" we routinely call "dilemmas." The book is not intended for easy questions, rather it is meant for tougher ones whose responses, if made in the spur of the moment, can easily lead to ethical flaws. Yet solving similar dilemmas can be seen as an integral part of leadership ethics, and ethical leaders set the appropriate contexts for acceptable ethical courses of action to take place. Although decisions made through such processes as the DIRR might not meet the full approval of all the parties involved, those resolutions would have the merit of being the result of applied wisdom, and of a thorough analysis that involves all stakeholders.

I have enhanced the process of DIRR by ending the analysis with a more practical undertaking understanding "prudent pragmatism" that Bluhm and Heineman (2007) proposed in their book *Ethics and Public Policy*. The caveat, however, stands in that these two authors purport to replace the classic foundations of ethics, understanding deontology, utilitarianism, and virtue ethics with their casuistic-type analysis of ethical quandaries. Additionally, they mean prudent pragmatism as an exhaustive method of ethical decision making. In this book, I have relied on the foundations of ethics to deconstruct the dilemma in question, and utilized prudent pragmatism in its practicality, including democratic consensus and compromise as key elements in the implementation stage of a course of action.

Reliance on the ethical foundations has caused my use of the African virtue of *kimuntu*, also referred to as *ubuntu* (Desmond Tutu, 2000). My interpretation of this concept meets Bujo's (2011) understanding that *kimuntu* means the African altruism or generosity as far as communal love and community building is concerned. Whatever metaphor or taxonomy I might use to identify this virtue will make it look nonexhaustive so profound is this concept. In itself *kimuntu* adequately presumes the presence of other virtues such as compassion, empathy, charity, and others. Bujo rightly calls it "this inalienable fundamental principle of African ethics" evoking the proverbial formula: "I am because we are, and because we are, I am too." It is worth mentioning that *kimuntu* or African solidarity does not mean the individual loses one's identity because of the community. Yet the individual is indispensable because each African subject is free to express his or her moral conviction while including the community. In this book, I implied that one of the major reasons why the African Diaspora remit so much to their countries of origin, whether or not they are entitled to vote, accounts for this *kimuntu* that is so engrained in their genes, so to speak. *Kimuntu* should come handy when African leaders can recall or use it in the context of the African "baobab tree" in debating the possibility to extend the rights to vote to the Diaspora.

The book also makes mention of a traditional African means of decision making mainly used in case of conflict resolution. The process bears many names depending on cultures and ethnicities, but it is commonly referred to as "African palaver" (Bujo, 2011), Mbiti (1999), African "village meeting under a big tree" (Ayittey, 1998), and African "baobab tree" by other people from whom I borrow the expression. Although those traditional meetings did not occur exclusively under a real baobab tree, many regions of Africa in fact don't grow that breed, it makes a great metaphor given the immense size and the age of that sort of tree whose shade can shelter a whole village and whose life can span hundreds of years. Somewhere in the book, I have equated the "African baobab tree" with Habermas' conception of the "public sphere," to emphasize the democratic character of such traditional gatherings. Sadly, modern political and African civil leaders hardly allude to this rich process and use it particularly to solve various matters. African leaders willing to tackle such issues as that in the current dilemma about the Diaspora rights to elections can find real inspiration in the African "baobab tree," which in fact requires the principles of ethical leadership I also address in the book.

What the reader would hopefully take away from this book is the emphasis on the importance of ethical leadership that comes handy in wisely solving daily individual, professional, national, and global dilemmas, which global leaders face. Likely the methodology applied in the case of the Diaspora rights to suffrage in home countries can be subject to adaptation and adoption across space, time, cultures, and academic disciplines. While the reader will familiarize himself or herself with the foundations of ethics, and other Global North concepts including prudent pragmatism and public sphere, the reader will gain insight into the richness of African traditions via some such analogous expressions as *kimuntu* and African "baobab tree."

Acknowledgments

This book is an outgrowth of an article of the same title I published in the *Journal of Third World Studies*. I express great gratitude to professor Harold Isaacs, the editor of the journal, for granting me permission to expand the article and include it in this publication. My gratitude goes particularly to the Lexington Publishing Company for supporting the publication of this book through their guidance and encouragement.

A special recognition goes to Most Reverend Mununu Kasiala, OCSO, my bishop and an authentic ethical leader, for his faith in my academic abilities. He has always requested that whatever I publish be translated in French for my home country audience. I hope his hope can be completed someday. I owe a debt of gratitude to Dr. Karen Bouwer, professor of French at the University of San Francisco, who gave me the encouragement and support I needed to complete this work. I owe a debt of gratitude to Gay Grymes, our UST doctoral student whose field research on the topic has greatly enriched the content of this book. My recognition goes to a promising global leader and doctoral student in leadership, Van Ngwa, and to Kelsey Aamlid, my graduate assistant, for lending a hand to the making of this book. The Honorable Pierre Buyoya, former president of Burundi for thirteen years, was so kind as to offer me a face-to-face interview for the purpose of this book. I owe him a great deal of gratitude for his openness and his friendship, as I do our mutual friend, the former Minnesota U.S. Senator, David Durenberger. I owe a debt of gratitude to Father David Smith, UST emeritus faculty, for his encouragement and editing of the earliest draft of this book.

A particular thank-you should be directed to Dr. Bruce Kramer for the inspiration I received from his book, but particularly for his love and friend-ship. Bruce embodies the principles of ethical leadership expressed in this book. He always treated his followers and collaborators, including me, with respect, honesty, fairness, and love whether he was the department chair for the Leadership, Policy, and Administration, the dean of the College of Applied Professional Studies, and finally the dean of the College of Education, Counseling, and Leadership. I always pray for him in his battle against ALS. I will always cherish his loving-kindness.

Never will I owe enough recognition to the Reverend Dennis Dease, the president of the University of St. Thomas, for his providential generosity. He is an ethical leader who has always treated others as he would want to be treated. A particular thank-you should be directed to my colleagues of the UST Leadership, Policy and Administration Department for their collegiality, trust, and encouragement. My gratitude goes also to Reverend Robert Niehoff, SJ, president of John Carroll University, OH, for his friendship and support.

I extend my gratitude to the cohorts of the International Leadership program, which I direct. May all of them find in this work my passion for the common good that I humbly communicate to the future global leaders they ought to become. My Ed.S students, particularly those from Lakeville, MN, as well my doctoral students in Minneapolis should be thanked for their understanding and appreciation of the foundations of ethics which they apply to concrete professional dilemmas.

I will always be indebted to these friends and family members: To Reverend Honore Kombo, *compagnon de lutte*, president of the first microfinance institution in Kikwit, my hometown, for his encouragement, advice as well as his unwavering friendship, which goes beyond brotherhood. To Theo Nana and the whole Nana family for being such a dependable friend and brother. May our departed friend and sister Bea Nzuzi find here the expression of our indefectible love, which we also share with her and our brother Professor Jacques Losso. To reliable friends Dr. Omer, G. Pasi, Frederic Wandey, Patric Kabangu, Marcellin Mbwamboma, Professor Guy Lucien Whembolua and Mianda Bashala, Professor Jack Mangala, Beatrice Isampete, Rev. Francois Xavier Eale, Matabisi Nicholas, Reverends Sebastien Bakatu and Jules Omba, Deo munianga, Bob and Paula Mankaka, Laure Kapita, Belange and Francoise Kaba, and the Mutombo and Mubwa families for their warmth, understanding and encouragement as if with my own family.

Finally, this list would be incomplete without mentioning my family members Sandra Bongila, Patricia and Paulin and Shaniya, Armand Ntantu, my sister Wivine, Fete Makyla, Narcisse Mungeye, my uncle Mulela and family, my uncle Olard Azangi and Ya Therese in Canada.

Introduction

An army of sheep led by a lion can defeat an army of lions led by a sheep.
—Ghanaian Proverb
Other people's wisdom prevents the king from being called a fool.
—Nigerian Proverb

A leadership ethics reflection on the African Diaspora and their rights to suffrage in their home countries is so timely that the European Conference on African Studies (ECAS) has convened a conference on this particular topic from June 25–28, 2013 in Lisbon, Portugal. A coincidence with the writing of this book could not be greater. In fact the ECAS conference is titled "Voting beyond Africa: African Migrants' Political Participation in the Electoral Processes of Their Countries of Origin." A book on the same topic seems overdue, which would get some attention at conferences of the same nature. More importantly, the conveners of the conference acknowledge the quasi complete absence of scholarship on the suffrage rights of the African Diaspora and call on scholars worldwide to ponder and share their findings. The following excerpt from the conference abstract strikes a chord:

> Since the 1990s, most African countries have started their democratization processes by organizing competitive multi-party elections. They have also granted external voting rights to their citizens living abroad. According to a report published in 2007 by the International Institute for Democracy and Electoral Assistance (IDEA), twenty-eight African countries such as Algeria, Kenya, Senegal or Rwanda now have external voting. These external elections provide insights into some of the strengths and weaknesses of the electoral process and of migrants' political transnational practices. Yet, the scholarship on this topic is almost non-existent (ECAS, 2013).

1

After going over the prospective conference sessions, I became convinced that my leadership ethics that analyzes from a global perspective the political as well socio-economic underpinnings of this topic would make an acceptable contribution to the missing academic research.

The question of "Why allow the expatriates to vote in the first place?" was tackled by Laurie Brand (2010) in her critical article "Authoritarian States and Voting from Abroad." To begin with, she examined various reasons why democratic countries would expand the right to vote to their citizens living overseas. Her findings revealed the following reasons: "ensuring that nationals abroad enjoy full (or fuller) citizenship rights" and restoring "respect for political rights" in the case of reemerging democracies. Then she addressed her major research question consisting of why then leaders of authoritarian regimes would expand their franchise to their nationals overseas? Reasons for the extension would certainly not amount to the spread of democratic process. Brand examined particularly three North African countries, Algeria, Morocco, and Tunisia, that have had authoritarian rules and extended their franchise to expatriates in the 1990s. Her finding revealed that those three countries portrayed their decision to extend the franchise as to "further development or deepening of citizenship," which amounts to some sort of politically calculated disguise. The real reasons for the extension, however, her research found, go as follows: those authoritarian regimes aim at cultivating emigrant loyalty; they purport to rally supporters who would eventually support their regimes in the event of economic difficulties; they are intent on exerting their sovereignty over their Diasporas. While deepening political participation stands for the main reason why democracies extend vote to expatriates, authoritarian states extend franchise as a stratagem aimed at strengthening the ideology and hegemony of their autocratic leadership.

This book is not about why the Diaspora vote (or does not vote), which entails a sound reasoning response at least as far as ethics is concerned. Nor does it regard how the expats are to vote, calling for a more logistical-like response. These two questions call for a clearer cut (black and white) determination that could fit the domain of political sciences from which Brand is writing or that of business management. Rather I am concerned with the leadership ethics question of whether the Diaspora ought to vote (in other words if it is desirable for them to vote) specifically in their homeland franchise. This question becomes even more complex when as in the case of Africa, some Diasporas participate in their countries' franchise whereas others don't. It implies and goes beyond the mere question of "why" or what the reasons are behind the fact that citizens of some countries vote and those of other nations do not vote. My concern is that of a grey area that belongs to the domain of ethics as this "subfield of philosophy that aims at clarifying the nature of right and wrong, good and bad. Besides clarifying the meaning and justification of ethical ideas, ethics tells us how we ought to behave" (Ingram

& Parks, 2002). In short, my analysis deals with whether it is right or wrong (good or bad; just or unjust; virtuous or immoral, desirable or undesirable) for citizens living overseas to be extended franchise, and for the leaders of African countries to extend the franchise to their Diaspora. Philosopher Immanuel Kant (1724–1804) argues that it is the duty of the ethical person (the leader) to treat others with respect. Kant's moral imperative on human respect has been at complete odds and hardly reconcilable with his stand on racial inferiority of Black Africans. On the one hand, Immanuel Kant disreputably wrote in his essay *Observations on the Feeling of the Beautiful and Sublime*: "So fundamental is the difference between [the Negro and White] races of man, and it appears to be as great in regard to mental capacities as in color" (Kant, 1960, P. 111). Various Kantian scholars add their voices of contempt to those of ethical leadership thinkers, including me, in decrying the inappropriate views Kant held of Black people. In particular, Thomas Hill and Bernard Boxill (2001), both defenders of Kant, disagree with his embarrassing and disparaging statement while pointing out that Kant unequivocally opposed slavery as wrong and not justifiable. On the other hand, in a formulation of the "categorical imperative," Kant's conception of respect gives people a command to "act so that you treat humanity, whether in your own person or in that of another, always as an end and never as a means only" (Kant, 1997, p. 46). Scholars agree that Kant's view of categorical imperative includes Blacks and Africans as agents of moral respect by virtue of their humanity. Laurence (2005) makes it explicit in his article "Moral Equality and Natural Inferiority" that Kant's categorical respect of humanity constitutes his official view of Blacks, whereas his visceral feelings about Blacks was a reflection of his actual position on the reality of things. Likewise Hill and Boxill (2001) made the same point that while Kant's moral philosophy says all the right things in making no exception regarding matters of race, his other writings often include controversial viewpoints. Concurring with Laurence (2005), I remain mindful of the tension within Kant's thought as a whole; I also echo the viewpoint of Hill and Boxill not to read Kant's objectionable non-moral writings into his ethical constructs. For example, Gregory Lewis Bynum (2011) in his essay "Kant's Conception of Respect and African American Education Rights" uses Kant's thought exclusively in its ethical dimension to examine African American education rights on three levels of the individual person's moral experience, the community as part of humanity, and the universal community of humanity as a whole.

The preceding discussion clears the ground for my use of Kant's ethical philosophy as I investigate the subject of the Diaspora Africans' suffrage in their home countries. The question remains as to whether the leadership of African countries would act with justice when facing the question of abroad vote. Northouse (2010) summarizes the five tenets of ethical leadership, which the leaders of African countries are called to apply as they face decision making in this particular question. Those principles of ethical leadership that underpin this work include building community, respecting others, serving others, manifesting honesty, and showing justice (p. 387).

The origins of the five principles of ethical leadership can be traced back to Aristotle, whereas their importance crisscrosses a variety of disciplines including bioethics (Judith, 2002), business ethics (Beauchamp & Bowie, 1988), counseling psychology (Kitchener, 1984), political ethics (Stuart, 1978; Thompson, 1987), educational administration (Fullan, 2003; Johnson, 2012), and many more. Based upon the five ethical leadership principles defined by Northouse (2010), which by no means claim exclusivity, it is safe to imply that the case of overseas franchise in this book presents a locus for a conceptual application of a typical ethical dilemma global leaders in various disciplines are likely to grapple with. The case in this analysis represents a tri-partite interrelation between the leaders, and their two respective constituencies of followers (homeland residents and citizens in residence overseas). This calls for global ethical leaders to act with respect toward their followers, serve their followers, show justice toward them, manifest honesty, and build community. These principles will be deemed applied with success when looking at them from the followers' perspective. For example, a nurtured people made aware of their own needs, values, and purposes will feel respected by their leaders; a people whose welfare is placed foremost in the leaders' plan would feel served; a people that sense they are in all fairness at the center of the decision making will feel treated with justice; a people to whom not only the truth is told, but also to whom leaders are open in their presentation of major issues regarding the country, that people will feel treated with honesty. The ethical leadership perspective applied in this dilemma does not rush to decision making without looking into the leaders' internal dispositions as suggested by Parker Palmer (1990) and above all without considering the benefit to those the leaders have the leadership obligation to serve, their followers (Greenleaf, 1977). No wonder the University of St. Thomas (UST) where I now teach has made the teaching and instruction of the "Intellectual and Ethical Foundations of Leadership" the very last and program exit course for most master's and education specialist (Ed.S) students.

Much of the inspiration for this book comes from the course I teach at the University of St. Thomas, MN, "The Intellectual and Ethical Foundations of Leadership." The course is designed for MA in international leadership, MA in leadership and students affairs, MA in leadership in public policy, MA in educational administration, Ed.S (Education Specialists), and doctoral students who choose to take it as an elective. An evaluation of the course brought the following comment from an Ed.S student—Lakeville, MN cohort:

If the day ever comes when I am the principal of an elementary school it will be my responsibility to lead in an ethical manner. . . . No matter what foundational approach I take when making decisions I will first need view the dilemma using the DIRR model. This protocol will be extremely helpful because it is an established process used by leaders to gain better understanding of an issue and provides clarity for how to proceed. First, it will be important to describe the issue at hand and take time to think about all of the key facts/ players and what brought about the dilemma in the first place. It will be important to then Interpret what has been happening along the way based on conversations, observations, and data. Next it will be crucial to take time to Rehearse, or in other words, think about all of the possible outcomes that could result from various scenarios. And finally, before any type of resolution or decision can be made I must Re-discern or re-frame the original dilemma. Doing so will allow me to reflect on the entire process because certain aspects of the dilemma could have changed along the way or perhaps certain viewpoints or perspectives were missed and not taken into consideration (UST Ed.S student).

A book on leadership and political ethics of the elections as pertaining to the African Diaspora is likely to attract the attention of many publics. The overall field of ethics will be much interested in the interdisciplinary approach of decision making utilized in this book. The particular context of African elections in general and the suffrage of the African expatriates in particular only presents a sample case analysis of leadership ethics decision making. Practitioners and scholars in several various disciplines might be interested in adapting this analysis process to their own professional cases. The methodology used to analyze the dilemma posed by the "rights to election of African Diaspora," Description (D), Interpretation (I), Rehearsal (R), and Re-discernment (R), represents a new trend, which is likely to captivate the interests of many ethicists. The majority of African Diaspora who advocate for their "birthright" to vote in their home countries will find here a balanced analysis. It is also my hope that African political leaders will be served here with some food for thought particularly when prompted to solve the question of whether to extend to rights to vote to their expatriates. Because transnationalism has become a fact of life in the current era of globalization, anyone interested in the global consequences of globalization can find benefit in this book. In effect, only in such a globalized world can the concern for abroad voting rise to the level of political, social, economic, and academic significance. Finally, instructors and students of international leadership and global affairs programs at the University of St. Thomas where I teach or elsewhere will find here an ethical analysis process they can apply to other global dilemmas.

Global leaders face problems every single day, but while many problems are easily solvable, some appear to be dilemmas. A dilemma can define as "a situation that requires a choice between options that are or seem equally unfavorable or mutually exclusive" or "problem that seems to defy a satisfactory solution." Some sages have metaphorically referred to solving a dilemma as making a choice to sit on either of a bull's two horns. Di-lemma from Greek: "two propositions" refers to a situation in which a choice must be made between alternative courses of action or argument. Kidder (1995) draws a contrast between what we commonly refer to as "dilemma," but is in reality a more or less easily solvable problem, and an ethical dilemma. He explains that a tough decision is one that a leader doesn't like making but knows must be made, whereas in a dilemma the problem has multiple choices of equal but different value. In the same lines, Ruggiero (2008) explicates that a *"moral dilemma* is defined as any predicament that arises from the impossibility of honoring all the moral values that deserve honoring. A moral dilemma exists whenever the conflicting obligations, ideals, and consequences are so very nearly equal in their importance that we feel we cannot choose among them, even though we must" (p. 124–125). The following case clearly exemplifies a classical dilemma in its conflicting ethical obligations and consequences; it calls for a resolution that an ethical leader must make although the leader is conscious that his or her chosen course of action might not meet universal consent. After pondering the ultimate distinction between a routine professional problem inappropriately referred to as "dilemma" in ordinary parlance and "ethical dilemma," an education specialist (Ed.S) student came to the following understanding:

> Although it seems like a very basic concept, the fact we spent so much time discussing the difference between problems and dilemmas was extremely helpful. I think many of us confuse the two terms because we assume the choices we face throughout our lives are dilemmas. However, I now realize most situations are nothing more than practical problems that need to be solved and once they are they typically turn out well with little or no ramifications. A dilemma, however, is one where the outcome will have an impact on others and there can be no "clear winner" so to speak. People making decisions will know they are faced with a dilemma when the choices they have to make will ultimately benefit some while neglecting and/or possibly harming others (Ed.S student, Lakeville, MN).

In traditional Africa, dilemmas, proverbs, and stories have been the backbone through which this originally culture of orality has carried on its education and mores. The example below intends to illustrate the African dilemmas' double purposes. First it presents the sharpness of an ethical dilemma and the quasi impossibility to provide a fully satisfactory code of action, such a tough question as opposed to easily solvable daily issues. Secondly, I use the dilemma below to make a point that African countries as well as their Diasporas are not foreign to the intricacies that ethical dilemmas present in a given society. In traditional Africa as well as nowadays, parents and sages may rely on insoluble dilemmas to enhance the moral and cognitive abilities of youth.

The more the reader is faced with the challenge to solve the dilemma, the worthier the ethical issue.

Once upon a time, a woman and her husband decided to leave their three small children behind and to walk across a three-hundred-mile jungle from the Congo to neighboring Angola in search of diamonds. The couple teams up with a friend who seemingly knows the way around to avoid falling prey to fierce animals or being caught by the notorious Angolan soldiers who patrol the borders. Angolan soldiers are particularly known for shooting Congolese returning from Angola with hidden diamonds, unless they strip themselves of their spoil and continue their way empty handed to the Congo. The three-month-pregnant woman and the two men carry heavy packs of goodies they intend to trade for diamonds with Angolan villagers.

Unable to trade the goodies they have carried, our three Congolese adventurers decide to dig a twelve-by-twelve-foot hole of about ten feet deep to sort out diamonds from piles of rocks, mud, and sand as diamond diggers do. This very extraneous endeavor has taken our adventurers six months to accomplish as they have gathered a sufficient amount of diamonds. The joyful couple had expected to purchase a new house, raise their small children in a decent manner, and take good care of the newborn. One way to safely hide diamonds from the Angolan soldiers is to swallow them, and recuperate them once past the borders. The woman's husband chooses to conceal the couple's share of diamonds in his stomach. Then the three people begin their trip back to the Congo with the woman now nine months pregnant.

Now they are in the Angolan borders; unfortunately for our travelers, they are apprehended by Angolan soldiers who demand that they surrender their diamonds, if any. When diamonds are in a stomach, they are nowhere to be detected. However, the couple's friend betrays them just to find his way alone to the jungle. As the lady's man is unable to present their share of diamonds, he is immediately executed in front of his wife who is left alone with the body of her husband. Ahead of her lays two hundred miles to cross alone in the dangerous jungle before she is able to join her now starving orphan children who have been expecting their parents' return for six months.

Worse, African tradition has it that you shall not mutilate the body of the dead, particularly that of your husband or wife at risk of incurring a severe curse that would leave the perpetrator outcast, schizophrenic, and totally disoriented. The devastated widow is left with impossible to no choices. She can either:

1. Tamper with her husband's body; cut it open, search his stomach, and recuperate the diamonds that would help secure her own life and the life of her children including the expected one. However, tampering with her husband's body seems dangerous given the severe conse-

quences of such desecration as prescribed and believed in African tradition. The woman will certainly be cursed, her life would get blurry, and she might even be unable to leave the jungle by herself. The curse will only procure psychological trauma, schizophrenia, and certain death.

2. Find her way back empty handed. If the woman is unwilling to try to desecrate the body of her husband, she will try to cross about two hundred miles of jungle alone, get back to her starving children, and live an even more stressful life without the help of her husband. This solution stands for a suicide since the woman is likely to give birth while trying to return to the Congo. Without telephone or hospital at her disposal, she is likely to fall victim to the jungle predators. Her chances to get human help in the wilderness are quite doomed. End of the story.

As presented, the two main potential courses of action represent both "horns of a bull" to sit on, and neither of them is conducive to an acceptable compromise. I confess that the story leads to an inconclusive solution, or a no-solution, whereas the dilemma of whether African Diaspora should vote in their countries of origin can end up with some consensus, though not universally acceptable. Instead of rushing toward a final course of action that can lend itself to an obvious falsehood, a careful analysis of the question seems paramount. However, I first propose to explore the genesis of the ethical case that will crisscross the book from "head to toe."

THE SPARK

Most ideas in the world find their origin from rather weird circumstances, and the thought of analyzing the right of the African Diaspora to elections in their countries of birth is not an exception. For those in the West, particularly in the United States who complain about the lack of interest in African news on the part of local and national media, the BBC has always been a reliable resource. As I went over different news topics on the African politics, a BBC survey struck a chord, so pertinent was the survey questionnaire it had addressed to Africans worldwide regarding the Diaspora's rights to local and national elections in their home countries. More intriguing was the disparity of responses to the seemingly simple question of whether or not the African Diaspora should/ought to vote in their birth countries. The short BBCs questionnaire goes as follows:

> As Uganda prepares to go to the polls, should its expats have the right to vote? So far almost a dozen African countries including Burkina Faso, Mali and South Africa allow their citizens living abroad to cast their votes. And Ghana

and Morocco are in the process of giving their expats the same rights. But in 2000, Zimbabwe stripped its nationals living abroad of their right to vote. With millions of Africans living outside the continent, should more countries give their expats the vote? Or when you leave your country, do you also leave behind your right to have a say in how the country is run? What impact would the diaspora have in your country's politics? (BBC News, 2006).

The more I read answers from the respondents who identified themselves by an online name and the country from which they were writing, the more it occurred to me that answering this apparently unsophisticated question was not as obvious as I first thought. Two particularly opposite responses caught my attention. Jean-Paul Muanda was the first respondent member of the Diaspora, originally from the D.R. Congo now living in Great Britain, who reacted in the following way:

> Recently the transitional government in DRC has refused the diaspora the rights to enroll and vote. I sense that they see a political threat and challenge in the diaspora community and therefore would like to keep them away as much as they can. However, this is wrong; diaspora can effectively contribute to the development of such a country. Preventing me from voting a leader of my choice would equal to an economic and political development suicide (BBC News, 2006).

Bazeyi, another member of the Diaspora, identifying herself as citizen of South Africa, responded in these words:

> "We African Diasporas are seeking our own success, getting permanent residence papers or citizenship in Western countries. Africans abroad represent a small population of the whole continent and their vote can't have an impact. The continent needs many things and most of them are more important than casting a ballot" (BBC News, 2006).

Both Jean-Paul and Bazeyi are members of the current African Diaspora, although they originated from different countries and their social, economic, and political conditions before and during their time in the Diaspora might somehow differ. However these and similar diametrically opposite positions regarding the right of the African Diaspora to elections in their countries of origin became so striking that it compelled me to investigate the question further. In fact, sixty percent of those responding to the BBC survey live in the Diaspora (Europe, Canada, or the United States); of them sixty percent favor their rights to vote in their countries of origin while the rest 40 percent oppose such a right. As I decided to tackle this question and come up with some resolution based upon a logically rigorous process worth replicating and adopting, I realized that I myself belong to the African Diaspora, though my understanding of the concept dated back to my years of secondary education and those of my teachings of the "Literature Noire Americaine" (Black American Literature) and "Negritude" in the D.R. Congo.

PERSONAL BACKGROUND ON DIASPORA

Diaspora was always a very remote word in my memory, which I first learned in my tenth grade of high school in the D.R. Congo in the 1970s. The term broadly referred to brothers and sisters that have been uprooted from the African land and brought forcefully in despicable conditions to European and American territories to work as slaves in plantations. I learned that Black African intellectuals put together a whole movement of self-consciousness of their African roots, identifying themselves as the African Diaspora, which for me meant vaguely a group of international exiles. This nebulous concept of Diaspora was later nuanced by my teaching of the same African American Literature to tenth- and twelfth-grade students in the 1990s. In my teaching I purposefully underscored the role of the leaders of the African Diaspora, such as W. E. B. Du Bois (1868–1963), Marcus Garvey (1887–1940), and Frantz Fanon (1925–1961), expanding the concept to encompass all Black Africans whose migration abroad was caused by the slavery trade. Although the Negritude movement or the recognition of own blackness aimed at blending the African motherland with its children living abroad, there was still a gap between the motherland and the Diaspora, at least as I conceived and imparted it.

Negritude began in the 1930s French colonies as a movement of resistance against colonization, by a group of intellectuals of African descent including Leopold Cedar Senghor (1906–2001) (later president of Senegal), Aimé Césaire (1913–2008) (Martinican poet), and the French Guyanese Léon-Gontran Damas (1912–1978). Theirs was the belief that to shake off the French political, intellectual and cultural hegemony, it was imperative to immerse in the shared Black heritage of members of the African Diaspora. In my teaching "Negritude" to Congolese high school students, I underscored that the Negritude movement grew and adopted oral and written literature as the main means of expressing the common frustrations and aspirations of Black people both on and outside the continent of Africa, using the word Diaspora to identify the second group. However, to me Diaspora remained an elusive reality that would resurface distractively even as I pursued my academic life in the United States in the 2000s. Soon the chaotic change of leadership in the D.R. Congo, resulting in the fall of the kleptocrat Mobutu and the ascension of the nationalist rebel Laurent Kabila, made me realize that I have not only crossed the threshold of the Diaspora, but also embraced the American culture while retaining my duties and rights as a citizen of Africa. The question of duties and rights of the African Diaspora never really crossed my mind until the turning of the political events in the D.R. Congo in late 1990s.

DIASPORA'S EXPERIENCE WITH ELECTIONS

In 1997, Laurent Kabila at the head of a mixture of rebels marched on Kinshasa, the capital city of the D.R. Congo, overthrowing Mobutu and installing another dictatorship. Kabila was known for his reliance on the Congolese Diaspora to fill key political and administrative positions of his new government. He considered himself member of the Diaspora after he had spent three decades in (1965–1997) in a self-inflicted political exile because of his opposition to Mobutu's regime. After learning about the regime change, and particularly the favorable attitude that President Laurent Kabila held toward the Diaspora members who returned home with sufficient academic backgrounds, many Congolese living abroad seized that opportunity to go back home. Such was the case of Mr. Fulani Mwamba, a Congolese member of the Diaspora who fled Mobutu's regime in the 1970s after his inflammatory writings put him at odds with the dictatorial regime. He had since found refuge in the United States, and welcomed the fall of the kleptocrat as a victory for the people and an opportunity for new social and political beginnings. In 1999, Mr. Fulani joined the bandwagon and went back to the Congo with the purpose to take over some political leadership position and educate his constituents in democratic processes, including free and transparent elections.

Although the regime of Laurent Kabila was favorable to the returning members of the Diaspora, the system was not yet open to democratic processes, as Mr. Fulani would soon learn the hard way. His political views and proclamations, and probably his writings, caused him to be arrested and incarcerated in conditions hardly humane. After about nine months in one of the most somber prisons in the D.R. Congo where his mental and psychological health began to deteriorate dangerously, the Congolese members of the Diaspora learned about his ordeal, contacted appropriate authorities, and obtained his return to the United States in extremis. Mr. Fulani had realized that although the Congolese Diaspora members could qualify to be nominated to some leadership positions in the country, their interference with the rights to elect country's officials such as the president or members of the parliament, or to be elected was a different beast. During his short reign up to his assassination on January 18, 2001, Kabila did not govern as a democrat nor did he officially attempt to initiate democratic venues for fair and transparent elections. The Diaspora was welcome to join the political system, not to question it or to exert any rights to elections. Fulani's story brought to another level my theoretical and practical understanding of the African Diaspora overall and its role in the political affairs of home countries.

Up to this point, there had been no incentive for me to explore deeply the question of how valuable an asset the Diaspora represents for a given continent, a country, or even a region of the world. The turning point would soon come. The African Studies Association (ASA) came up with a call for proposals for its 53rd Annual Meeting in San Francisco (December 12–21, 2010) under the title "African Diaspora and Diasporas in Africa." The story of Mr. Fulani and several other leaders of the African Diaspora who intend only to participate honestly in the political design of their homelands began to strike a chord in my academic psychic. As my eagerness to decorticate the phenomenon of African Diaspora grew, so did my reluctance to engage the political role that Africans living abroad ought to play in their countries of origin. Such a topic seemed reasonably too broad and less attractive in addition to the fact that many other scholars more competent in political sciences or similar disciplines have tried to dissect it. Like for any major event in our human life, the turning point and the decision time came when I came across British Broadcasting Corporation (BBC) News' survey on whether the African Diaspora ought to participate in local elections of their home countries. The time was ripe for me to examine a question that had matured with my academic inroads, but that I had been putting off in the back of my mind. While the context of Mr. Fulani's political involvement would have certainly be overwhelming to analyze, the theme proposed by the BBC survey appeared to be more manageable. The BBC News with its online publication of a survey destined to African Diaspora only offered me a chance to consider a more in-depth analysis of the topic. In substance, the survey revealed that African governments, as well as the African Diaspora are divided as far as the rights to elections in their home countries are concerned. Any researcher coming across a topic of this nature would first ask: how do I approach this question? Specifically, my question became: how do I analyze the issue of "Ought African Diaspora to vote in their home countries?"

HOW TO APPROACH THE SUBJECT?

One would argue that the issue of political elections, that of African Diaspora, ought to be approached with methodologies pertaining to political science and political sociology, or at best political ethics. For *Webster's New Collegiate Dictionary* (1974), political science defines as "a social science concerned chiefly with the description and analysis of political and especially governmental institutions and processes" (p. 890). In his book *Contemporary Political Sociology: Globalization, Politics and Power*, Nash (2010) contends that political sociology "has to be seen as concerned, above all, with relations between state and society . . . Political sociology directs attention toward 'the social circumstances of politics that is, how politics both is shaped by and shapes other events in societies. Instead of treating the political area and its actors as independent from other happenings in society, [political sociology] treats that arena as intimately related to all social institutions.'" Finally, political ethics has to do with good action, dealing specifically with acting ethically in politics. Political science, political sociology, and political ethics deal with the apparatus of political bodies whether within society, between different constituents of society or within the governing body of a state nation. They might analyze elections as an element of politics within the limits of their scope, but they would not provide a broad and encompassing study of elections in the international contexts of the African Diaspora. A more appropriate analysis of this question requires an interdisciplinary, ethical, and international approach of the socio-political relevance of external elections for both the African societies and their people living outside of their borders. Worth mentioning are various studies on the politics of running elections in Africa, although none of them treats specifically the issue of the Diaspora's rights to elections. For example, Lindberg (2006) in *Democracy and Elections in Africa* studies 232 elections in forty-four African countries, extending Rustow's (1970) theory that democratic behavior produces democratic values. The Electoral Institute of Southern Africa (EISA) has specialized itself in political analysis of the electoral processes in Africa. This organization has produced numerous studies, such as *From Military Rule to Multiparty Democracy: Political Reforms and Challenges in Lesotho* (EISA, 2003), *Elections and Democratisation in Malawi: An Uncertain Process* (EISA Research Report, 2005), and *Multiparty Democracy and Elections in Namibia* (EISA Research Report, 2005). Additionally, such organizations as International Institute for Democracy and Electoral Assistance (IDEA) and the Electoral Knowledge Network offer a considerable body of literature and comparative studies suggesting systems that may provide a closer connection between parliament, government, and potential Diaspora voters (AfriMAP, 2009). IDEA has dedicated extensive research on the structure and running of external voting, including elections procedures pertaining to African Diaspora. It might well provide key information for countries that are considering implementing external voting processes for their expatriates. In 1998, IDEA established a project called "The Administration and Cost of Elections" (ACE, 2010) designed to offer a range of services related to electoral knowledge, assistance, and capacity development. The ACE website is a major source of comprehensive information and customized advice on electoral processes.

In spite of providing significant sources of analysis on the running of worldwide democratic elections, these specialized organizations, EISA, IDEA, and ACE, don't come up with a framework to study the foundational issue of whether or not African Diaspora hold the right to vote in their home countries in the first place. As I pondered various approaches to resolve this political dilemma, leadership ethics came handy. James Fieser (2009) in *The Internet Encyclopedia of Philosophy* (IEP) gives a workable definition of ethics, identifying it with "moral philosophy." For it, "The field of ethics . . . involves systematizing, defending, and recommending concepts of right and wrong behavior." I have been teaching a graduate course titled "The Intellectual and Ethical Foundations of Leadership" for MA students in administration leadership, leadership and students affairs, leadership policy and international leadership, as well as doctoral students at the University of St. Thomas. The Department of Leadership, Policy and Administration for which I teach prides itself for its interdisciplinary approach and its teaching premised on a blend of academic theory and professional practice to make the learning relevant to our students who happen to be professional leaders. Since the inception of the certificate and MA in international leadership in 2008, currently under my direction, interdisciplinary learning instruction has been a cornerstone of our curriculum, which blends elements of political science, economics, history, and educational leadership, all nuanced by theories and practices of ethics.

Against this backdrop, it became obvious that the dilemma of whether African Diaspora might hold the right to vote in their countries of origin would be best solved using a combination of disciplines as only leadership ethics can garner. Ciulla in her *Ethics, the Heart of Leadership* (2004) rightly maintains that the nature of leadership is interdisciplinary, and this book concerns socio-political leaders whose influence and decision impacts directly or indirectly African Diaspora from within and/or from without. In *Meeting the Ethical Challenges of Leadership*, Johnson (2012) explains that "leaders are change agents engaged in furthering the needs, wants, and goals of leaders and followers alike. They are found wherever humans associate with one another, whether in a social movement, sports team, task force, nonprofit agency, state legislature, military unit, or corporation" (p. xix). In the same token, the politicians who make electoral laws in Africa, the African expatriates who contribute their remittances in their home countries, the international community that has vested interest in Africa by virtue of our global fate, and the international leaders-to-be and other individuals contemplating a visible or tacit role for the sake of Africa, all have various degrees of leadership roles to play.

Simply put, ethics concerns itself with judgment as to whether human behavior is right or wrong (Johnson, 2012). Ethics allows us to place a judgment on individual, professional, and even legal behaviors. We are appalled by the idea that some cultures had regulated that if a woman gave birth to twin babies, they should be left to die on a top of a hill for fear of bringing their ancestors' curse to the whole humankind. Such despicable customary practice at all times does not preclude the fact that cultures that practiced the killing of twinborn maintained the highest moral standard of life preservation. On the one hand the execution of innocent twin babies was an utmost repulsive act, on the other hand the spirit of the cultures that practiced the abominable act was rooted in the moral principle that life is to be preserved at all cost, and any maleficent agent that goes against social life ought to be eliminated. Therefore we find ourselves in a shaky ethical ground from which to judge those cultures as unethical because they were impelled by their belief systems and the contexts of their primitive societies. However, we are called to condemn the actions of leaders, who decide to steal from the public coffers while their people are starving, who intimidate members of opposition parties for speaking up against unfair practices, and who resort to amend the constitution of their countries in order to maintain themselves in power. Considered the above, I see it an ethical decision for one living in both African and Western cultures, like myself, to discern the case brought before me by whether Africans outside their home countries should actively take part in domestic elections. Since the subject to study has been clearly enough conceived, I pondered the better methodological approach to examine a question that offers complex contours in international leadership, politics, and ethics.

Enomoto and Kramer (2007) propose a practical methodology of analysis of ethical issues in various contexts. Although their tackles primarily leaders in education settings, its substance can be adapted to solve dilemmas in such diverse domains as political ethics and political sociology. In many instances, this book goes beyond a mere application of the methodology proposed by the two authors. First it expands the locus of the analysis to the international arena whereas Enomoto and Kramer addressed the school administration leadership of the United States only. Second, it breaks away from the boundaries of educational leadership or administration leadership to tackle sociopolitical issues hardly analyzed with ethical standards. Third, this book adopts and expands the concept of "prudent pragmatism" (Bluhm and Heineman, 2007) originating from Habermas' "public sphere" or "communicative action." In itself, prudent pragmatism implies and encompasses Dewey's (1976) notion of democratic decision-making or democratic leadership that Enomoto and Kramer believe to be the ultimate goal of their ethical process. They define Dewey's concept of democracy "as the razor line of space between the needs of the individual and the needs of the group or groups to which the individual belongs. This means that effective leaders recognize the importance of balancing individual needs with group needs" (p. 73).

Enomoto and Kramer's (2007) method is a reflective process beginning from the description of a dilemma and ending with action while cycling back again. Figure I.1 presents the fourfold methodology revolving around Description, Interpretation, Rehearsal, and Re-discernment (DIRR). Referring to qualitative methodologies, Description is the first step of the ethical analy-sis, which includes exhaustive details of the situation, the environment, the location, and the people involved in the dilemma. Information should answer such questions as what is at stake, who is involved, when and where did it happen? The second step of this ethical analysis is Interpretation, an explora-tory attempt to theorize the dilemma by means of ethical language. It is also an identification of tensions among ethical standards. It inquires: what of the universal values versus desires, or what of the personal life/interest versus public life/interest is at issue?

For example one side considers the constitution of a country as a set of laws or rules to be upheld at all times, and another side feels that the articles of the constitution are guidelines subject to interpretation; there is ethical conflict between universal rules and contextual interpretation of the rules. To reveal the tensions represented by the problem, Interpretation calls for the examination of what is virtuous for individual members versus what is virtu-ous for the group or whether it is the question of duty versus utility.

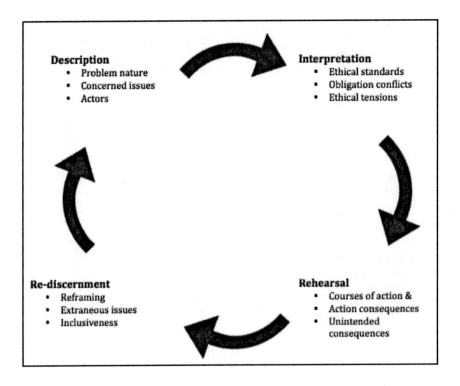

Figure I.1

The third step in the DIRR is Rehearsal, consisting of laying out all possible courses of action, meaning all decisions that can be taken as a result of the dilemma analysis. Enomoto and Kramer (2007) maintain that the above analysis of the tensions between ethical standards prepare the leaders to predict what might occur given the wants and desires, as well as the duties and responsibilities of those in the decision making. Also carefully scrutinized would be the positive and negative consequences, including long-term and short-term outcomes of each possible course of action. The last step of this ethical process is called Rediscernment as it requires that the leader reframes the dilemma in a more vivid and creative language, such as a simile, a metaphor, and other visual techniques. This step presents a synoptic view of ethical tensions, consequences, and possible decisions; it also includes all viewpoints giving them due consideration in resolving the dilemma in question. More importantly, Rediscernment or the revision of the picture of the dilemma might prompt the leader to consider extraneous elements that can heighten the chances of consensus and compromise. Consensus refers to reaching out a better understanding of the situation before taking action, and compromise points to the middle ground entailing the loss or win of something by the parties involved.

ORGANIZATION OF THE BOOK

Chapter 1 discusses the concept of Diaspora in general and the African Diaspora in particular. Since the connotation of the terminology is nuanced by time and space, it is critical to design the boundaries within which the analysis of this book operates. After a workable meaning of Diaspora has been determined, chapter 2 describes in detail what the dilemma is that the right to elections in the Diaspora's home countries poses. Chapters 2 through 5 follow the process of construction, deconstruction and reconstruction proposed in Enomoto and Kramer's (2007) methodology of ethical analysis. Chapter 3 examines the dilemma of the Diaspora's election in the lenses of duty-based ethics or deontology. The question stands as follows: Ought African Diaspora to vote in their home countries? Chapter 4 uses desired-based ethics or utilitarianism to analyze the dilemma in terms of the outcome of the Diaspora's election. The question here comes down to: does the electoral process in favor or against African Diaspora produce the greater good for the greater numbers? In chapter 5, I examine the concerned dilemma in the light of virtue ethics as proposed by Shapiro and Stefkovich (2011) in their *Ethical Leadership and Decision Making in Education*. In chapter 6, I address the ethical conflicts or tensions that can arise as a consequence of siding with one or multiple ethical standards when analyzing the dilemma of African Diaspora's right to elections. This leads us to chapter 7 in which I rehearse possible resolutions to the question and address the consequences of each potential course of action. Chapter 8 is a review of major issues involved in the process of decision making. It tackles extraneous facets of the question that might have been otherwise left untouched or unexamined. In chapter 9, I use prudent pragmatism as presented by Bluhm and Heineman (2007) to harness a resolution of the dilemma based upon a two-way communication. Chapter 10 concludes this sample ethical analysis of a case of interest for international leaders, that of the African Diaspora right to elections in their countries of origin.

While only a dozen African countries grant their citizens living abroad the right to vote, the remaining nations fall between those that have unimplemented vote provisions for their expatriates and the countries that have yet to consider such provisions. Although some members of the Diaspora support the right to elections, others oppose it; however, both the African countries and the Diaspora welcome the significant financial contribution of the Diaspora as a citizen right or a duty, yet they fail to regard the right to vote as an integral element of citizenship. The split among African countries and African Diaspora poses the following ethical dilemma: How can African Diaspora carry the expectation due to citizens to invest in the economy of their birth countries while they are being deprived of the citizen right to elect the leaders of the same countries? To analyze this question, I will use an "inquiry method for working ethical dilemmas" proposed by Enomoto & Kramer (2007) in their book *Leading through the Quagmire*, and I will suggest a "prudent pragmatism" resolution as laid out by Bluhm and Heineman (2007) in *Ethics and Public Policy*, advocating for the Diaspora's rights to invest in both the economy and the governance of their birth countries. A global leader might find here a balanced process to adapt when facing ethical dilemmas in the international spectrum.

Chapter One

Understanding African Diaspora

If I do not remember you,
let my tongue stick to the roof of my mouth;
if I prefer not (my homeland) above
my chief joy.
—Psalm 137:6 (Adapted)

Palmer (1998) rightly states that the concept of diaspora is too broad to be confined to the peoples of African descent alone. Other historians, such as Harold Isaacs, professor emeritus at Georgia Southwestern State University, and Palmer himself, are familiar with the migration of Asians that occurred between ten and twenty thousand years ago, resulting in their crossing the Bering Strait and settling in North, South America as well as in the Caribbean islands. Also well known and better studied is the migration or Diaspora of the Jewish people, which began about two thousand years ago. The migration of Muslim peoples started eight centuries ago with the process of bringing their religion and culture to various parts of Africa, Asia, and Europe. In the fifteenth century, European people began their own penetration of the African continent, which resulted in their dispersal in several other parts of the world including the Americas. These diasporic streams or migrations of specific people are complex in their timing, impetus, direction, and nature, and they contribute only to the challenge to come up with a single understanding of what a diaspora really stands for.

Since many scholars (Manning, 2009; Okpewho, 2009) concede that the word "diaspora" can bear various connotations dependent on the contexts of its usage, this chapter will narrow down the meaning of this broad concept to a more manageable and pragmatic unit of understanding. The present chapter funnels, so to speak, various understandings of the concept of diaspora from its etymology through its applicability in the African historical context to

19

nowadays imageries of what is referred to as "African Diaspora." Instead of focusing on the plain historicity of the Diaspora, I will engage in the question of why people of African descent who recognize their origins from the motherland of Africa consider themselves as part of the current Diaspora. With this in mind, the chapter turns to provide a glimpse of what has been broadly considered as diaspora before analyzing the socio-economic and political basis of people of African descent who have been forced by diverse forces to live away from their homeland, or who have otherwise chosen to conduct their existence outside the land of Africa. The following will be our guiding questions in this chapter: what does "diaspora" mean? What do scholars say about African Diaspora? Why do people of African origin who have migrated in the countries of the Global North perceive themselves as members of the African Diaspora? What are the workable characteristics of African Diaspora that would allow for an ethical and leadership examination?

THE MEANING OF "DIASPORA"

"Diaspora" is an ancient word (Gilroy, 1993) originating from the Greek language to refer to the dispersion or scattering of a people away from an ancestral homeland. The term "Diaspora" has been long used to refer almost exclusively to the dispersion of Jewish people around the world as enshrined in the book of Deuteronomy (28:25). History has it that the dispersion of Jewish people originated from their captivity in Babylonia where they were kept in slavery, then they spread between their homeland in Palestine to Mesopotamia and to the shores of the Mediterranean Sea. The following lyric renders well both the agony of captivity for the Hebrews during their exile in Babylon and the indefectible memory of their motherland:

> By the rivers of Babylon
> There we sat down and there we wept
> When we remembered Zion. . .
> On the willows there we hung up our harps
> For there our captors asked us for songs,
> And our tormentors asked for mirth, saying
> Sing us one of the songs of Zion
> How could we sing the Lord's song in a foreign land?
> If I forget you, O Jerusalem, Let my right hand wither!
> Let my tongue cling to the roof of my mouth
> If I do not remember you, If I do not set Jerusalem
> Above my highest joy
> (Ps. 137, 1–6).

Around 200 BCE, when the Hebrew Bible was translated into Greek, becoming the Septuagint, the term "Diaspora" was used to express the scattering of the Jews outside their homeland. The term "Diaspora" moved with the Jewish as they continued to willingly or unwillingly scatter through Europe, North Africa, and Asia (Manning, 2009). From an essentially religious reality of being uprooted from one's "holy land," the word "diaspora" has adopted social, political, and anthropological meanings over time. Its essential features, however, have always encompassed the forced displacement of a given people as well as the indefectible remembrance of their beloved motherland. Another historical reference to Diaspora is made in relationship to Black Africans since the beginning of the sixteenth century's slavery trade when Africans were forcibly uprooted from their native lands. Although most of those Africans transported as slaves to North America, South America and the Caribbean were captured from West Africa, countless other African men and women were traded in Central and Southern Africa (Manning, 2009). As it happened with the Jewish early Diaspora, the Black African movement of the slavery period (fifteenth–nineteenth centuries) was not voluntary. Rather, it was the result of inhumane triangulated trade that treated Black Africans as raw resources to sell, buy, and manufacture. Scholars have estimated that as many as twelve million Black Africans from West Africa alone were sold into slavery and exiled into the new world during the four hundred years of legalized slavery trade (Braziel & Mannur, 2003). Like the Hebrews, the African slaves yearned to return home, so unbreakable were their umbilical ties to their mother Africa.

Olaudah Equiano's (2007) autobiography is also a story of this affective connection to the native land and the yearning to return home. Before Nigeria became known as a country, Olaudah Equiano was a year-old child who was kidnapped from a village of the same region. After his capture from somewhere in Southern Nigeria, Equiano was shipped across oceans and seas in atrocious conditions, and sold into slavery in the West Indies, North America, and in England. His continual prayers for freedom took years before they were answered. He suffered humiliation, loneliness, homesickness in addition to the betrayal of those he considered "good masters," and the devils who treated him worse than a dog. He survived not only battles and shipwrecks but also the attempts of certain Americans who managed to kidnap freed slaves. He educated himself socially through his experiences of domestic and mercantile servitudes in the three regions he crossed as a slave. Eventually he was able to achieve prominence and respectability particularly within British society. Fortune took him to the service of two young ladies who taught him Christianity. He eventually learned good English, reading, writing, and navigation. Having earned enough money by bitter toil, he was finally able to buy his freedom in the West Indies and returned to England. Eight years before his death in 1797 at age fifty-two, Olaudah Equiano, known to Europeans as "Gustavus Vassa," published his autobiography. In conjunction with several indigenous British citizens, and other Africans who had earned freedom from slavery, he contributed all he could to the efforts that eventually led to the abolition of slavery. Unfortunately, Equiano did not live to see how abolition would take effect. He had hoped to return to Africa, particularly to the new establishment of the settlement in Sierra Leone to which other freed slaves were repatriated. The opportunity to return to his motherland was denied him because of differences with the organizers of the slave-repatriation project. The truth is that despite the passage of time and the intervention of the European outlook on life, Equiano affectionately clang to his African sensibilities.

In *Theorizing Diaspora*, editors Braziel and Mannur (2003) posit that the word "diaspora has been increasingly used by anthropologists, literacy theorists, and cultural critics to describe the mass migrations and displacements of the second half of the twentieth century, particularly in reference to independence movements in formerly colonized areas, waves of refugees fleeing war-torn states, and fluxes of economic migration in the post–World War II era" (p. 4). According to these authors, theorizations of diaspora have been marked by ambiguities. Diaspora denotes communities of people that have been displaced from their homes of birth via migration, immigration, or exile. Often those displacements have been the consequences of colonial expansion. According to Hall (cited by Braziel & Mannur, 2003), "the diaspora experience 'is defined, not by essence or purity, but by the recognition of the necessary heterogeneity and diversity, by a conception of identity which lives in and through, not despite, difference; by hybridity'" (p. 5).

AFRICAN DIASPORA

"By 'African diaspora,' I mean the Americas and also the islands of the Atlantic and the mainland of western Europe. Each of these three regions has its own history, but these histories are tightly connected. For instance, Africans first came to Europe as part of the Old World diaspora, but as the Atlantic slave trade grew, Africans came to Europe especially by way of the Atlantic" (Manning, 2009, p. 4). While acknowledging that the application of the term "diaspora" to the dispersed people of African descent is subject to many assumptions, Manning posits that the term might have been coined and used for the first time in 1965 at an African conference hosted by the University of Dar es Salaam in Tanzania. This happened two decades after the end of WWII and the creation of the state of Israel, when analyses of Holocaust and the history of the Jewish people brought to the forefront the memories of the Diaspora. In Africa and the Caribbean, however, this was the time of country independence, of self-determination, but also the time to bring about the memories of all African people scattered around the world, all forming the African "Diaspora" in analogy to the Jewish dispersion. Manning's analysis of African Diaspora focuses on the connections that hold together the African communities whether within or outside the continent of Africa. He makes the point of studying the African Diaspora in its relations with non-African hegemonic powers and non-African communities. While the African connections to the global diaspora on which Manning focuses has its merit, I theorize that a sustained relationship of affection between the people of African descent living abroad and the motherland via individual visits and socio-economic participations is an important feature of the African Diaspora. In "*The African Diaspora: African Origins and New World Identities,*" editors Okpewho, Davies and Mazrui (1999) discussed, among other themes, the potential origin of African Diaspora. They note that although such authors as Ivan van Sertima (in his *They Came before Columbus*) and Vincent Bakpetu Thompson (in his book *The Making of the Africa Diaspora in the Americas 1441–1900*) provide evidence of a plausible arrival of Africa in the Americas before Columbus, both authors do not come up with a substantial explanation. Against this backdrop, it is safe to agree with Okpewho, Davies, and Mazrui on the sixteenth century as the era during which Black Africa began their massive dispersion toward the Global North countries of Europe, Australia, and America. Although this book uses the 1600s as informal origination of the global African Diaspora, it does not preclude the movements of Black people within and outside the continent from the birth of humanity.

In 1324, Musa, then the *mansa* or emperor of the Mali Empire, set out for a long travel in the company of an important entourage. Not only did he cross the northern boundaries of his empire, he traversed the Sahara desert, joining with many other pilgrims from the savanna country, all heading to Mecca for their pilgrimage to the *hajj*, the most sacred place in Islamic faith. Musa's caravan was so imposing that it encompassed hundred of camels, many of them loaded with an impressive quantity of gold dust for gifts and trades. Reports have it that his expenditure was so extravagant that the Egyptian currency, the dirham, was forced to devalue. Upon his arrival in Mecca, the emperor Musa joined other pilgrims from around the Muslim world in walking seven times around the Kaba in honor of God, Abraham, and the prophet Mohamed. After losing the majority of his camels in Mecca to the cold, the emperor was forced to buy more for his return. On his way back, struck for cash, he stopped in Egypt and borrowed money from merchants, which he reimbursed upon his arrival in Mali. The story of this famous emperor is only an illustration of countless other movements of people before and after the 1600s African Diaspora. Manning (2009) reports that before 1600 Africans experienced a history of connections and changes beyond the continent, which led to exchanges of individuals, ideas, and conquests. History tells of the many trades that occurred between Portuguese and African kings, including the principalities of the kingdom of Kongo in the fourteenth century.

Aboard Portuguese vessels, African sailors traveled as far they could work, such as in India, Japan, the Mediterranean, and the Caribbean.

A more accurate timeline of the African Diaspora has always been subject to discussions and conveniences. For example Okpewho & Nzegwu (2009) provide a thematic dissection of the diaspora in three paradigms representing three eras or phases. The first phase identified as the *labor imperative* is characterized by the labor imposed upon the sons and daughters of Africa by the West. This era would include the slavery trade which caused the decimation of millions of Africans in the process of passage from their homeland to the Europe, America, and the Caribbean. Phase second of the African migration is identified as the era of *the territorial imperative* in which the United States through the Monroe Doctrine allowed the colonization of Africa, contributing to the scramble of Africa. The author quickly concedes that the United States itself did not directly maintain direct imperialism on colonized countries of Africa. The author calls the third phase of African Diaspora the *extractive imperative* in reference to the rivalries between Africa and the West over African minerals in the postcolonization epoch. Okpewho's division of the African Diaspora is exclusively, like the whole book *The African Diaspora: African Origins and the New World Identities*, centered on the United States in addition to its lack of well defined historical periods that would track the migration of Africans over history. Also left out are the valiant members of the African Diaspora in other corners of the world, such as Europe, Asia, and the Caribbean.

Against this rather restrictive notion of the African Diaspora presented by Okpewho & Nzegwu (2009), Manning (2009) posits that "the African diaspora refers initially to the world of black people" (2009, p. 7). Whereas Palmer (1998) specifies that African Diaspora encompasses

> the millions of people of African descent living in various societies who are united by a past based significantly but not exclusively upon "racial" oppression and the struggles against it: and who, despite the cultural variations and political and other divisions among them, share an emotional bond with one another and with their ancestral continent; and who also, regardless of their location, face broadly similar problems in constructing and realizing themselves (p. 3).

Palmer warned that his definition of the African Diaspora does not include a sustained desire to immigrate to Africa. Such people of African origin as the Rastafarians, freed slaves, and thousands of African Americans, who left for Ethiopia and particularly Liberia in the nineteenth century, have advocated for a return to Africa. This idea was maintained by other individuals, for instance Henry Highland Garnet (1815–1882), Henry McNeal Turner (1834–1915), and Marcus Garvey (1887–1940). However, the African continent as a place to reestablish roots has faded away over time. Palmer rightly points out that the study of modern African Diaspora must entail the study of the home continent. Additionally, because the modern African Diaspora is different from that of the Black American, Black British, or Caribbean diaspora, Palmer (1998) contends that scholars ought to apply methodologies that are adapted to the modern—twenty-first-century—socio-cultural environments in which people of African descent find themselves.

In his article "The African Diaspora," Palmer (2000) denounces what he perceives to be a confusion that many scholars make between diaspora and migration. Migration, he posits, refers to a movement of a people within and/ or outside its polity whereas diaspora suggests several migratory streams of a people to many destinations. He implies that the concept of African Diaspora should be used only in reference to the Atlantic slave trade, "which resulted in the movement of the Ibo peoples of contemporary Nigeria to Jamaica, South Carolina, Cuba, Barbados, and so on" (p. 3). While Palmer rejects as ahistorical the notion that the African Diaspora equates merely to "Africans abroad," he avoids the logical reasoning implying that one is not a member of the African Diaspora unless one's ancestors forcibly migrated to the Global North as a result of the slave trade. Such reasoning would have excluded from the African Diaspora millions of people from African descent who have migrated to Europe, the United States, and Australia in circumstances other than the Black slavery trade.

Aside from the above controversy, Palmer (2000) makes an important distinction between what he calls the "pre-modern" and the "post-modern" African Diaspora. The pre-modern Diaspora includes three streams, which were overall voluntary:

1) The movement out of the continent beginning 100,000 years ago, also referred to as the great exodus
2) The movement of the Bantu-speaking peoples starting 3,000 BCE
3) The diasporic stream of the fifth century BCE, toward Asia, Europe, and the Middle East

The modern African Diaspora encompasses also three major movements of African people (Palmer, 2000). The first movement is associated with the Atlantic slavery trade of the mid-fifteenth century; the second stream consists of the movement of African slaves toward Asia around the sixteenth century; the third movement consists of the migration of Africans and people of African descent in several countries of the world. As noted above, this last movement of African people or "Africans abroad" constitutes the focal point of this book. For the purpose of this book, I understand the Diaspora more like social scientists "to refer to migrants who settle in distant lands and produce new generations, all the while maintaining ties of affections with and making occasional visits to each other and their homeland" (Manning, p. 2). What then are the characteristics of such a "modern" African Diaspora?

Chapter 1

CHARACTERISTICS OF AFRICAN DIASPORA

The term "African Diaspora," as I understand it, encompasses both the descendants of Africans that were made slaves and forced to move to Europe and the Americas via the Atlantic slave trade, the largest population having been brought to Brazil. However, the term, understanding modern African Diaspora, has to apply in particular to Africans who have emigrated from their home countries for such reasons as education, employment, and living security for themselves and their offspring. In 2010 the World Bank (2010) identified about 140 million Africans, the majority originated from sub-Saharan Africa, living in the Global West countries of Europe and the Americas, as well as in Australia. This important number of people has the propensity to revitalize Africa both economically and politically.

   Whether they had been dispersed through slavery or migration, the African Diaspora I am concerned with in this book first acknowledges the presence of a homeland, ordinarily a country or a territory internationally recognized. Second, members of the identified Diaspora have kept emotional ties with the country of origin, usually characterized by presence of kin in a mother country, frequent contacts through individual or group visits, social media contacts, and knowledge of an ethnic language. Third, there exist economic contributions through NGOs, businesses, and cooperative or individual remittances. Fourth, there is active participation in political clout in host countries and significant influence in one's homeland's political arena both regarding issues of Diaspora concern and of domestic interest. This fourth attribution of the African Diaspora might also include lobbying nationally or internationally on behalf of the homeland. Broadly put, the recognized membership of the African Diaspora can sum up to social, economic, and political affiliations with homelands. While the homelands with Diaspora are often conflicted in both their loyalty to the people living within their boundaries, whom they ordinarily prefer, and those living abroad, the Diaspora is more broadly concerned with transnational issues benefitting home countries as a whole. For the purpose of this study, I have made the determination to limit the application of the African Diaspora to its political dimension as it interacts with economic, social, and cultural aspects that might impact decision making in general, and the right to vote in homelands, in particular. Legitimately, my working definition of African Diaspora might include all descendants of Africa, particularly those with more recent ties to the continent and who have fully adopted both their African and host countries. Specifically, this book is interested in the relationship of relatively recent immigrants from Africa to their native countries and its political and social systems. To further narrow the scope of this inquiry on leadership and political ethics, this work targets the African Diaspora or expatriates whose countries of origin recognize as citizens by law.

Understandably, Diaspora leaders might find themselves caught up in a conflict of dual loyalties between their homeland and the host state. In a book chapter, Shain & Wittes (2002) provide one example of loyalty conflict:

> [When] the Bush administration in 1991 threatened to withhold loan guaran-
> tees to Israel unless Israel agreed not to spend the money in the occupied West
> Bank and Gaza, Jewish-American advocacy organizations were forced to
> choose between their good relations with the U.S foreign policy establishment
> and their loyal support of Israeli polices in its conflict with the Palestinians.
> Most chose to support Israeli policy at the cost of incurring the wrath of their
> American partners. But after the bilateral U.S.-Israel confrontation was re-
> solved and the loan guarantees were put into place, many of those same organ-
> izations joined the effort to pressure the Israeli government to adopt a different
> attitude toward settlement activity in the West Bank and Gaza (p. 189).

The above example is suggestive of the complication in analyzing the African Diaspora's right to election in their home countries given that most of them might hold multiple citizenships, and are therefore torn between loyalties to two polities. Although subject to controversies, the African Un-ion (AU) sees African Diaspora as consisting of people of "African origin living outside the continent, irrespective of their citizenship and nationality and who are willing to contribute to the development of the continent and the building of the African Union" (The World Bank, 2010). An estimated 169 million people from African origin live in the United States, Canada, South America (Brazil, Colombia, and Venezuela), the Caribbean, and Europe, whose ties with Africa are limited to economic development alone per the AU standards. Although all the expatriates can broadly identify themselves with the Diaspora for economic reasons, the lack of a direct ongoing affilia-tion with current African nations would exclude many people living abroad from access to the political realm.

A working understanding of African Diaspora refers to "migrants who settle in distant lands and produce new generations, all the while maintaining ties of affection with and making occasional visits to each other and their homeland" (Manning, 2009). Although ties of affection with countries of origin are not a condition sine qua non for economic linkage, they must constitute an essential element for seeking and being granted political rights for those in the Diaspora. Matibe distinguishes three types of African expatri-ates in the Diaspora: first political—those who left because their lives were in danger; second, academic—those who left for further education; and third economic—those who left for financial reasons (Matibe, 2009). This taxono-my operates under the assumption that political refugees and exiles lose their right to elections because of their obvious opposition to the established polit-ical leadership of their countries of origin. Braun and Gratschew, however, state that four main groups of people living abroad are entitled to vote: the migrant workers, refugees, "individuals in certain professional groups such as military personnel, public office and diplomatic staff (and their families)" and the Diaspora on a temporary or permanent stay abroad (Braun & Gratschew, 2007).

The book implies the question of who is a *citizen.* Are the children of guest workers citizens of their parents' home country? How about the children of political refugees? How about the grandchildren? In this book I use citizenship in its contemporary usage "to refer to the legal relationship between an individual and a state, in which the state recognizes and guarantees the individual's rights" (Manby, 2009, p. ix). Explicitly, the book is concerned with the African Diaspora or expatriates whose countries of origin recognizes as citizens by law. "Few African countries provide for an explicit right to a nationality (citizenship). Moreover, though the laws in more than half of the continent's countries grant children born on their soil the right to citizenship at birth or the right to claim citizenship when they reach the age of majority, the observance of these laws is often lacking" (Braun & Gratschew, p. 1).

Chapter Two

Describing the Dilemma

"To Caesar what is Caesar's, to God what is God's."
—Gospel of Matthew, 22:21
"One cannot serve two masters. He would love one and hate the other."
—Gospel of Matthew, 6:24

Can the African Diaspora vote in both their host countries and their home countries? Can the African Diaspora pay taxes to both their host countries and their home countries? Can the African Diaspora serve two masters: their host countries and their home countries, without loving one and disowning the other?

Rushworth Kidder (1995) refers to dilemma as a problem that has multiple choices of equal but different value as opposed to a tough ethical decision, one that a leader does not like to make but knows must be made. Some scholars treat a dilemma purely as a problem that presents multiple choices of equal value. For example, since Senegal allows for its citizens living abroad to vote, provided they travel either to the country or to assigned voting booths in pre-determined cities of the United States, it might be a tough decision for Senegalese to take an expensive trip and vote. In this case the concerned individuals have only two simple choices: travel for vote and not travel. However, the question of whether the expatriate Senegalese ought to vote on socio-political decisions by which they do not abide in their home country where they no longer reside—but pay millions of dollars yearly in remittances—such a question becomes an ethical dilemma. "No matter what decision is made, it feels like a lose-lose situation. Here the case becomes an ethical dilemma where the choices might not be optimal or might require compromise among all involved" (Enomoto & Kramer, 2007). For a question of this nature, the answer cannot just amount to "yes, the African Diaspora ought to vote in their home countries" or "no they should not vote at all."

Many countries with active Diasporas are grappling with the dilemma of their rights to elections.

In 2007, the Jamaican *National Weekly* (2007) published an article under the title "Should the Diaspora Vote, or Not?" Although the article leaned toward denying the Diaspora's participation to the electoral process, it showed serious reservation as to cut off a right, which citizens living abroad perceive as a natural endowment. Both sides of the dilemma are well expressed by this Jamaican member of the Diaspora: On the one hand,

> not because we are members of the Diaspora, and through the structured development of this Diaspora have what seems to be a stronger link with the home country, does this make it possible for us to partake in the elections of that country. The real fact is that we gave up our right to actively participate in the political process of that country when we decided to leave it. Sadly, we cannot enjoy the best of both worlds, and moreover, the constitution of the country we left may not allow us to have this enjoyment. Maybe those who are opposed to those in the Diaspora voting by absentee ballots are right. Those in the Diaspora left their natives lands to seek after a better life, while those remaining had to endure through thick and thin. What then gives the Diaspora the right to direct the lives of those back home with their votes, since they are not experiencing life there (*National Weekly* 2007).

The second side of the dilemma states as follows: "But on the other hand, does the fact that one left their native land in search of a dream preclude them from having an active interest in the country in which they were born, raised, and where they want to return someday?" (np). I acknowledge that this question could generate a monster of a debate, which the Diaspora needs to address rather urgently so as to reach a "definitive solution." As the saying goes, a dilemma offers the choice of "sitting on either horn of a bull"; neither one offers a real comfort. It follows that the question is more complex and requires an elaborate analysis based upon an ethical process of decision making, which must begin with a clear description of the dilemma. I will describe the polarities of the Diaspora right to homeland's elections at the national and individual levels.

POLARITY AT THE NATIONAL LEVEL

While only a dozen African countries grant their citizens living abroad the right to vote, the remaining nations fall between those that have unimplemented vote provisions for their expatriates and the countries that have yet to consider such provisions. Additionally, the BBC's survey reveals a struggle many Africans in Diaspora are grappling with. On the one hand, explain Navarro, Morales, and Gratschew, the African Diaspora from such countries as Botswana and Cape Verde participate in both the economy and the politics of their respective countries of origin via regular remittances and organized elections (Navarro, Morales & Gratschew, 2007). They are entrusted with full citizenship, bearing a voice in both the economic and political realms of their countries. Mercer, Page, and Evans noted that remittances disbursed either through organized associations or family ties entitle members of the Diaspora to full citizenship (Mercer, Page & Evans, 2008). They see the right to vote as giving them the power to shape their countries' destiny in terms of governance and good leadership.

On the other hand, Navarro, Morales, and Gratschew (2007) indicate that African countries, with the exception of twenty-eight, do not have provisions for external voting. Other countries with external vote provisions still never implemented them. Of those twenty-eight countries, some never acted on abroad voting (Navarro, Morales & Gratschew, 2007). For example, Angola has unimplemented external voting provisions, while Ghana only allows diplomats and a few international organizations' workers to vote. For such countries as Lesotho, Mauritius, South Africa, and Zimbabwe, only citizens in official missions abroad of a diplomatic and military nature can vote. Other countries restrict entitlement to an external vote according to the length of stay abroad, ranging from one year to nineteen years. This category includes Chad, Guinea, Mozambique, and Senegal.

The International Institute for Democracy and Electoral Assistance (IDEA) (2010), reporting on the electoral processes in Africa, states that twenty-four countries out of fifty-eight hold personal elections for the Diaspora, in which members are allowed to show up at polling stations or polling sites to cast their votes (IDEA, 2007). Two countries hold postal elections, consisting of completing ballot papers and returning them by post to officials in charge of conducting the elections. Two countries conduct expatriates' elections by proxy, a process by which qualified electors formally appoint other persons to vote on their behalf. Twenty-three countries do not have elections for their expatriates and two countries are transitioning from no-election status to some suffrage for their expatriates. The only flip side of personal voting is the potential difficulty for the Diaspora members to make the trip to voting locations, particularly if they are situated at unaffordable distances from the members' residences. In this case, however, both the provision for and the implementation of abroad voting exists in the twenty-four countries that use the personal voting method. The same can be said of postal and proxy elections. In the first case, the ballots might arrive late at the compiling point whereas there is no control over proxy electors as to whom they would really cast the vote for.

Far from critiquing the voting methods assigned to the African Diaspora, many proponents of the Diaspora rights to elections would contend that the implementation of expatriate suffrage, whatever its imperfections, is praiseworthy. Twenty-five countries out of fifty-eight, including those transitioning to a suffrage process for the Diaspora, such as the Democratic Republic of the Congo and Eritrea, don't have a provision for the Diaspora election. These are likely to find the analysis contained in the present book relevant should they consider discussing this burning topic in the next future. However, the significance of the book as far as the political ethics leadership is concerned extends to all the fifty-eight countries in their dealing with whether their Diasporas ought to vote in local elections of home countries. A well discerned decision in this regard might even consist of reversing a decision previously made on this issue. For example, South Africa which allowed its expatriates to vote in the general elections of 1994 had to pull the provision back in the subsequent elections of 1999 and 2004 claiming irregularities. However, only some months prior to the 2009 general suffrage, the Constitutional Court of South Africa ruled that South Africans living and working abroad who were registered voters could vote in the country's general elections in April 2009, after notifying the SA's chief electoral officer of their intention to vote before a set deadline (Mbola, 2009). More than 16,000 South Africans, out of over two million living abroad, cast their ballots at overseas stations, with record numbers in Canberra (Australia), Dubai (United Arab Emirates), and Willington (New Zealand) (SouthAfrica.Info, 2009).

The following countries don't have any provision for external voting: Burkina Faso, Cameroon, Comoros, Democratic Republic of Congo, Egypt, Eritrea, Ethiopia, Kenya, Liberia, Libyan Arab Jamahiriya, Madagascar, Malawi, Mauritania, Morocco, Nigeria, Republic of the Congo (Brazzaville), Reunion, Saint Helena, Seychelles, Sierra Leone, Somalia, South Sudan, Swaziland, Tanzania, United Republic of Uganda, Western Sahara, and Zambia. Of these countries, three (D.R. Congo, Eritrea and Somalia) are transitioning to a potential external vote, whereas Angola holds an unimplemented external voting provision (IDEA, 2007). Although officially known for implementing their external suffrage, such countries as Ghana, Lesotho, Mauritius, and Zimbabwe restrict entitlement to an external vote according to activity abroad. For example Ghana extends the right to vote abroad solely to such people as diplomats, employees of the international organizations or the United Nations, Ghanaian peacekeepers, and student beneficiaries of scholarship from government (IDEA, 2007). Additionally, some African countries restrict entitlement to an external vote according to the length of stay abroad. Such is the example of Chad which requires the elector to be enrolled in the consular registry six months prior to the electoral process. Guinea has a limit of nineteen years of living abroad, after which one cannot vote. Mozambique requires a minimum stay of one full year abroad before one registers as an external voter. For Senegal, the Diaspora member should stay a minimum of six months in the jurisdiction of Senegalese diplomatic representative abroad before registering for vote. Given all the restrictions aforementioned, the pool of the African Diaspora members allowed to exercise electoral rights from their host countries can be estimated to a third of the African expatriates in age of voting. The below examples of Ghana and Mozambique only illustrate how most African countries stand diametrically opposed with regard to their Diaspora's right to local elections.

Ghana stands out as an African country that has been polarized around the Diaspora's right to national suffrage. For memory, Ghana gained independence from Britain in 1957, becoming the first country in sub-Saharan Africa to shake the colonial yoke. Since 1981, the transition of power from the ruling party to the opposition has been traditionally very peaceful avoiding the country some violence that has plagued other countries in the region, such as Cote d'Ivoire. Ghana has scheduled both the presidential and national assembly elections on December 2012. Its general legislation of the electoral framework integrates the legal provision regarding voter registration (Holtved, 2010). Although not mandatory, voting registration is established as a right, which according to the law, must be done in person at registration centers. The Electoral Commission of Ghana reserves the rights to determine the modalities for registration and define each citizen's eligibility. The general criteria for eligibility stipulate that the applicant must be a Ghanaian citizen, eighteen years of age or older, of sound mind, ordinarily a resident of the electoral area where the applicant wishes to vote, and allowed by law to register for the elections. Citizens on duty outside the country are allowed to vote by proxy in two conditions: they had registered in advance and indicated the person who would vote on their behalf. However, Ghanaian expatriates have neither access to registration nor to voting. As summarized by Kofi Ellison from the Ghanaian Diaspora, numerous political, social, personal, and ethical reasons can be evoked to keep the Diaspora out of the suffrage process: "There is a heavily politicized debate currently ongoing in Ghana. Usually, it was the government in power that would oppose the right of diasporans to vote. However, it is the main opposition that is concocting all sorts of reasons to oppose the Diaspora vote. I personally will not vote!" (BBC News, 2006, p. 1).

As opposed to Ghana, Mozambique stands out as a country benefitting from the Diaspora's right to local suffrage. Mozambique gained its independence from Portugal in 1975, battling civil war, economic mismanagement, and famine up to 1992 when a peace deal ended a sixteen-year civil war. Its population was estimated at twenty-three million in 2009, of which an average of 200,000 citizens are expatriates (UN, 2009). Nanitelamio (2007) notes that both voter registration law and the general elections law of the country support the right to local elections of its citizens living abroad. For example, the country's electoral laws stipulate that registration for elections and referenda in Mozambique should be conducted both within and outside the national territory (Article 9 of Law no. 18/2002 of October 10, 2002). According to Article 10 of the General Elections Law no. 7/2004 of June 17, 2004, as presented by Nanitelamio, "Mozambican citizens registered abroad are eligible for the elections foreseen in the present law" (p. 59). Additionally, provisions of Article 11 with regard to Mozambican expatriates demands that registered members of the Mozambican Diaspora cast their vote at identified diplomatic and consular missions. The 2004 presidential and legislative elections recorded a lower turnout of Mozambican expatriates. For the proponents of the abolition of the Diaspora elections, the insignificant numbers of registered electors stood up as a sufficient alibi. However, when compared with the national turnout of thirty-six percent, Mozambican Diaspora did well in Africa (fifty-seven percent) and sixty-four percent in the rest of the world, reinforcing the conviction that Mozambican expatriates deserve to maintain their right to elections in their homeland. Rationale for grating Mozambican Diaspora rights to elections is grounded on national unity particularly because of the socio-political role expatriates played in their fight for independence and in quelling subsequent rebellions. To the nation building premise should also be added Mozambican Diaspora's significant contribution to the socio-economic fabric of the country through financial remittances.

Ghana and Mozambique only exemplify the divergent positions African countries hold vis-à-vis suffrage laws, policies, and practices. My contention, however, is not to forward a recommendation that all countries in Africa ought to harmonize their electoral laws and policies one way or the other. Rather the rationales of either country, both in favor and against allowing external votes, underscore further the two polarities—or the two horns or a bull—of the dilemma, and the subsequent difficulty to solve it.

POLARITY AT THE INDIVIDUAL LEVEL

The World Bank estimates that thirty million Africans have immigrated in the Global North within the last three decades. According to Obiagali Ezekwesili, the World Bank's vice president for Africa, African Diaspora remits an estimate of $32–40 billion annually to the continent, exceeding the official foreign aid to the region (Fleshman, 2010). However, many African expatriates originate from countries that allow exclusively economic trades with their Diaspora. Other countries restrict the right to vote to selected members whose sole reason for being in the Diaspora amounts to official missions. African Diasporans are believed to hold the irrevocable duty that is a cultural expectation, to improve the economy of their countries, but have no right to influence the political outcomes of elections or other governing activities. Even the African Union (AU) perceives the Diaspora as a fellowship of economic citizens when it calls for its children abroad to assist in the economic development of the continent without mention of the influence the

Diaspora can exert on its leadership (Manby, 2009). A significant part of the African Diaspora argues that the duty to invest economically in their countries of origin should go hand in hand with the right to designate the leaders of those countries. They feel even more uprooted, disenfranchised, and used for holding only half of the power required to reach a sustainable development in those countries. Some go as far as to claim the right to be voted for (Manby, 2009).

In an article titled, "Ghanaians in the Diaspora Also Want to Vote," Stephen Queye (2011) states that their Diaspora has demanded to exercise the right to vote. Given that the Diaspora has been making substantial contribution to the economy of the country via remittances, they deserve to also partake to the political life of the country. In fact Ghanaian Diaspora contribute a minimum of four billion Cedis to their motherland every year representing the third largest contribution source to the economy of the country. Writing in favor of the diasporic Ghanaian right to local elections, Kwaku Kyem (2005) summed up his constitutional and legal argumentation in three major premises. First the Diaspora's entitlement to home suffrage originates from Ghanaian constitutional right "to live, vote, be recognized and treated as such, guaranteed by Article 6(2) of the 1992 Constitution stipulating that: subject to the provisions of this Constitution, a person born in or outside of Ghana after the coming into force of this Constitution, shall become a citizen of Ghana at the date of his birth if either of his parents or grandparents is or was a citizen of Ghana." Second, the first president of Ghana, Dr. Kwame Nkrumah, led the country to its independence upon his return from a study abroad. The country counts numerous returnees, such as Dr. Nkrumah, who have assumed successful political positions. It stands that extending the right to vote to the Diaspora would prepare valuable members to participate in the domestic politics. Third Ghanaians abroad already exert some sort of political influence in the country through the various contributions to the local political processes, in spite of the lack of opportunity to affect the collective choice at home and of a possibility for self-determination. Furthermore, many instances have urged the Diaspora to actively exert political influence on the country for instance when some members accept political appointments by the government and decide to return home and serve.

In the contrary, a few among the African Diaspora, including many from countries that grant the right to vote, believe they do not deserve such a right for various reasons. Some claim that without paying taxes in their countries of origin, they would cheat had they elected country leaders (BBC News, 2006). Others feel strongly about clinging to the right to vote in countries where they don't intend to live anymore, particularly if they also hold citizenship in their country of adoption (Manby, 2009). Added to this group are those citizens living abroad whose countries of origin had decided to revoke the right to vote they had previously enjoyed. For example in 2005, Zimbabwe's Supreme Court ruled that one had to reside in a particular constituency (within Zimbabwe) at least for a year prior to the election date (Tungwarara, 2007). Taking all the above into consideration, the dilemma states as follows:

If the Diaspora does not vote, it stands as a second class citizenry, holding only the duty to provide to the economic needs of their countries. It remains stripped of the power to make systemic change in their country of origin. Additionally, without influence in the politics of the country, even the remittances the Diaspora pays to the government might be misused for lack of real accountability. However, if the Diaspora is granted the power to vote it will interfere in the political affairs of a country they do not live in any longer, and to which the majority pay no taxes. Their vote might be more detrimental to the development of the country, because they would not know where current politicians stand on real social issues. In addition, external voting processes come with the risk of double voting, "such as voters casting a vote both from their home country and from abroad" (Braun & Gratschew, 2007, p. 4).

To provide concrete illustrations to this subject, I directed Gay Grymes, a current doctoral student at the University of St. Thomas, MN, to conduct a qualitative study on the African Diaspora's political involvement in native countries. Marshall and Rossman (2006) posit that "qualitative research is a broad approach to the study of social phenomena" (p.2) purporting to uncover meanings people assign to their experiences. Scholars in the qualitative inquiry tradition often use phenomenology as a way to describe meaning for several individuals of their lived experiences of a concept or phenomenon (Creswell, 2012). This investigation of the involvement of African students in the politics of their countries involved in-depth interviews, field observations, and probing questions. Five students of African birth who are currently living in the United States participated in the study. Although the small size of participants as well as the specific contexts of their home countries may not be representative of a whole continent of Africa, an in-depth study of a phenomenological nature allows to gauging the shared feelings and lived experiences of a given population. Qualitative researchers agree that a study that looks deeply into the characteristics of a very small sample often results in more knowledge than a study that tackles the same problem by collecting only shallow information on a large sample (Borg and Gall, 1983). Participants in the study originated from the sub-Saharan countries of Liberia, Cameroon, Somalia, Ethiopia, and Uganda. The study collected evidence through semi-structured interviews (Merriam, 2009) consisting of enforcing some loose consistency in questions while allowing for additional probing of diverging answers in order to uncover the participants' unique experiences, beliefs, and feelings. Throughout this book, I have cited and quoted the evidence gathered from the five participants in the study to support the dichotomy of views earlier presented in the BBC interviews (2006), which the Diaspora Africans hold toward political elections in their home countries.

Of the five immigrants Gay interviewed in the Minnesota Twin Cities, two are particularly polar opposite in their views on the Diaspora's role in their country of origin. Obviously the two stories recount individual experiences, each with specific contexts and circumstances in which their migration to the United States occurred. Their stories encompass many commonalities with those of other Africans who have moved to various corners of the Global North. For confidentiality reasons, the names of the interviewees have been kept secret, but I will identify them by the pseudo first names of Brian and Samuel. Brian whose native land is Liberia fled the country in 2003 shortly before the resignation of Charles Taylor who had ruled over Liberia since 1997. After the killing of his brother by Taylor's regime Brian, whose opposition to the corrupt regime was made public, was forced to flee the country and find refuge in the United States. Asked why he would not return home to actively engage in politics, he contended that he fears for his life since most of those who executed his brother under the previous regime have never been brought to justice. Instead they still work in the current government as members of parliament and in other higher positions. Responding to the question of "tell me more about your participation in the electoral and political process of your native country," Brian responded as follows:

> When I was in Liberia I served as the assistant commissioner of motor vehicle division of the Ministry of finance and I was actively involved in student politics. When I was in school I voted twice in my life during the Charles Taylor regime and the Samuel Doe regime and I was involved in mobilizing people to go and vote for their conscience and vote for those who they feel, not tell them who to vote for. I told them to vote for those who they feel could make their lives better and the country better. Choices were made and Samuel Doe was elected and they saw the results. . . In the results for the 2005 election I wasn't in the country. I was in the United States. I am a US citizen. . . but I am a Liberian first and foremost I can't forget that that's where I came from. . . I have some students (in Liberia) that I have personally helped economically that I send money to keep them in school. . . God has given me this opportunity so I send one or two or three hundred dollars home a month to help them. Secondly my parents and my siblings are there, and all of them are in school. So I help them also. That money helps to fuel the economy. Every dollar that we send, there was a report once that said millions of dollars are wired by Liberians back to help fuel the economy. That's my involvement socially and economically in Liberia (Student Interviews).

To the question of "are you still a citizen of Liberia? Can you have dual citizenship?" Brian responded:

No. . . That's why I am fighting. . . because we don't come here on our own accord. We were forced out of our country. And I have come. I took advantage of the opportunities. I have whatever I need. I am educated. And then to go back and invest whatever, give back to my country what my country gave me, but the opportunity is not there. . . The US encourages dual citizenship. There can be Israelis who are US citizens, Arab Israelis who are Americans, Mexican American. . . they go back home because it is their countries. But I don't want to go to a country where I will not be welcome, where I was born, my ances- tors are buried, my parents are there, I have a house, I have a birth certificate that says I was born there. But they ran me out and said "no you cannot come home" (Student Interviews).

Given the opportunity to bear dual citizenship and return home, Brian would joyfully join the bandwagon of the expatriate Liberians willing to make a political dent in their native land. His desire to participate in Liberian local elections is reflected in the only political activity he can exert from abroad: encouraging his siblings and friends that still reside in the country to engage fully in the electoral processes, including voting. From his own account, Brian's reasoning for holding the right to vote in his native Liberia goes as in the following premises:

1. As a born citizen of Liberia, I have an innate right to participate in the electoral process within my country.
2. Although I am no longer physically present in the country, I contribute to the social-economic sustainability of the country through such so- cial activities as financial remittances.
3. In my view, my engagements in both the social development and the political process of my country are interwoven filial obligations that entail each other.
4. Therefore, I am obligated to participate in the social-economic ad- vancement of my home country; therefore I am obligated to decide on policies and leadership of the country.

As opposed to Brian's position that is held by many Africans living in the Diaspora, stands the view of numerous Africans both at home and in the Diaspora who see a potential disposition for the Diaspora's election as an aberration. Samuel's story, collected by our Ed.D. student at UST, is an account of such a denial:

"Tell me about your participation in the electoral or political processes of your native country: Somalia."
No, I was not involved. I came here young. My father stayed away from politics. And in Somalia, mostly people. . . follow the footsteps of their father. My father was an agriculturalist. He worked with the World Bank; he was a PhD from Colorado State University. In fact, in 1983 when my father saw that [the country] was deteriorating to the point where the military was instituting a

grab of everything, my father felt insecure about the situation and that was the time that he decided to bring his family out. So, growing up, I always wanted to follow my father's footstep and, you know go in to agriculture and focus on food security for the people. So, in politics, I have not got involved. . . I think my first consciousness of politics back home was around 2000. . . that's when I really felt that the country needed young and more open-minded people that can have the head to see beyond the clannish mentality. So I was the first people who formed Somali Student Association, University of Minnesota at the time when I was going, and our aim was to focus on the young children, those who were graduating, and have families here. And so we felt like . . . if we can change here in the Diaspora, and create new mentality so those back home who are receiving support from their locals, they won't be cut off. And those were the most important for us because our aim was to let the Somali people know that. . . we are absolutely different from the rest of Africa. And it's sad because now we provide the worst case of example for Africa instead of the best because Somalia is one of few countries in Africa that has the same language, same religion, same background. . . to now say, "Look, Somalia, who shares all these common things, are killing themselves." It's really sad. . . To make it short, I think. . . I was too young to get involved in Somalia, but until today, I don't really see [myself] involved in politics. . . I am a very kind-hearted individual and I don't have the guts to be in the political process but I am in the human rights. . . in the social justice, and I believe we make corrections to those, so the political process can be better. . . Yes I am a US citizen, my family is US citizens. And I am a Somalia citizen. Somalia has a rule like if you're from Somalia, you will always be Somali. About not taking part in elections, people in Somalia would say about the Diaspora members "You guys did not take part of the problems of this country; you were not here; you escaped, you really were not part of us for this long. To come back and say 'We will help you rebuild the country.' Do you really know enough about our problems?" (Student Interviews).

On both sides of the continent, opponents of the Diaspora's right to elect native lands' officials increasingly base their argument on the failure for citizens living abroad to pay taxes to their home countries. No African country requires its Diaspora to pay taxes on incomes earned outside the country. Those opponents argue that both citizens living in Africa as well as the expatriates contribute to the socio-economic welfare of their countries via remittances and income investment in their home countries. Furthermore, most members of the Diaspora earn higher incomes than the median incomes of those remaining in home countries that pay national and local taxes. Because "rights must come with obligations," opponents of the Diaspora's rights to elections hold that citizens dwelling on the continent hold the right to vote and determine how they are to be governed given that they fulfill their responsibilities of paying taxes for their governments' operations. Therefore, they argue, expatriates must not demand the right to vote in home countries as long they do not meet the responsibility of paying taxes to run the operations of the governments. This argument was used by the government of Zimbabwe to revoke its Diaspora's election right on the grounds that it did not comply with the obligations of paying taxes (BBC News, 2006). Simply put, this reasoning stands as in following logical premises:

1. The right to vote in a given country is interrelated with socio-economic obligations including paying taxes, sending remittances, and living the political implications of the policies voted on.
2. The reality of being born in a country is not a qualifying criterion for holding the right to vote in a home country.
3. A country citizen must hold both the rights to vote and the responsibilities pertaining to the governing of the countries.
4. Members of the African Diaspora pay remittances whenever they see fit, but do not fulfill the patriotic obligation of paying taxes to the governments of their home countries. Therefore, members of the African Diaspora cannot vote in domestic elections of their countries of birth.

In this chapter, I have laid out the polarities of the dilemma posed by the realization that twenty-eight African countries out of fifty-eight have no provision or have not implemented their lethargic policies for the Diaspora election. National as well as individual rationales in favor and against the suffrage rights of the African Diaspora have been described in some great details. That thirty million Africans who have migrated to every nook and corner of the world within the last three decades do not vote in their home countries where they hold ties of affection via socio-economic contributions is a matter of a close ethical analysis. Proponents of the Diaspora election right claim that it is ethically unfair to celebrate the economic development contributions of the African expatriates to their countries while denying them the rights to vote in local elections. Opponents of the diasporic right to suffrage retort that it is equally unfair for such as the 30,000 Africans with PhDs who have caused the continent's brain drain and enjoyed a better education and life in the West to decide by way of elections on policies and leaders they are not familiar with and under which they will never live.

With this controversy in mind, I move to the next chapter, which will begin what Enomoto and Kramer's ethical methodology identified as the "interpretation" of the dilemma. Enomoto & Kramer (2007) posit that the interpretation and analysis of a dilemma should consider whether "the situation is based on mutually exclusive beliefs among participants or groups" (p. 99) or whether there exist universal duties or desires at issue. This calls for an ethical analysis based upon the two classic standards referred to as deontology (or duty-based ethics) and utilitarianism (or desire-based ethics). These two ethical standards can't be more enshrined in the case of the African Diaspora, some of whom consider voting in their countries of origin as an inherent right, whereas others maintain that interfering in such intimate political matters will be a disservice to the people.

Besides the popular standards of utilitarianism (or consequentialism) and Kantianism (or deontology), different ethicists have proposed different categories of interpretations often positioning themselves between the two classic views. Shapiro and Stefkovich for example propose a kaleidoscopic analysis of a dilemma consisting of applying a multidimensional approach centered on their "ethics of professionalism" (Shapiro & Stefkovich, 2011). In the following I will somehow kaleidoscopically interpret the issue of the African Diaspora right to elections, considering both classic views, the ethical obligations that might conflict, and other standards such as virtue ethics, ethics of care, and ethics of justice and of critique (Starratt, 2004). The next chapter will interpret the dilemma presented by African Diaspora rights to election in deontological standard.

Chapter Three

Diaspora Vote in Duty-Based Ethics

This chapter aims at exploring whether people of African descent who have established themselves in countries other than those of their birth hold the universal right or the duty to participation in national suffrage in their home countries. Before engaging the subject, it pays to keep in mind the leading questions of: what is duty-based ethics? How can duty be understood in African ethics? How would a so-called "universal duty ethics" or deontology apply to the contexts of African Diaspora? And how would the application of such an ethical principle elevate the judgment of a global leader faced with a similar question?

> The right to vote does not depend on whether one is rich or poor; it depends on citizenship. And all citizens have equal rights—check the constitution(BBC News, 2006).

Duty ethics or ethics based upon deontological or universal system of judgment largely refers to the work of the German philosopher Immanuel Kant. Kant has been known as the proponent of deontology or duty-based ethics, which involves one's respect of obligations or duties (Bluhm & Heineman, 2007). Knowing a little about his life will help understand Kant's ethical philosophy. Born in Konigsberg, Germany in 1724, Kant died in 1804 in the same city whose surroundings he never left. Short in stature, Kant was a quiet man and such a methodical personality that, according to one tradition, the inhabitants of Konigsberg set their watches at 3:00 PM every day when Kant took his walk. While he lived a single-man life, he basically devoted his existence to the study and teaching of philosophy at the University of Konigsberg. His magnum opus, *The Critique of Pure Reason,* published in 1781, propelled Kant as one of the greatest philosophers of his time. Most scholars agree that his duties-based ethics is mostly encapsulated in his *Fun-*

damental Principles of the Metaphysics, published in 1785, which is regarded as one of the most important books in the history of ethics. Its basic
premise posits that "a moral action is done out of a sense of duty" or obligation "rather than as a result of following one's inclinations or desires" (Enomoto & Kramer, p. 8). Simply put, Kant's system is called deontology, in
other words based on following rules. The word "deontology" itself is drawn
from the Greek (*deon*, "duty") to characterize individuals who tend to make
decisions based upon strong beliefs with a sense of responsibility, and a
commitment to meet expectations according to prescribed set of rules. For
Kant, those rules are absolutes, in other words, considered universal as they
must apply without exception to any single person in the face of the earth.
Kant appealed to the sole reason, as opposed to a higher being such as God,
in stating that humans possess absolute duties. Kant does not imply that such
people who believe in God like the majority of African Diaspora are not
ethical, but the universality of the duty he maintains applies to universally to
all humankind whether or not they hold a belief in a Transcendent. Ingram
and Parks (2002) make it more explicit as they explain that "a duty is something that you are required to do whether you want it or not. It means that no
matter how you feel about it or what you want to do, you must do that act:
whether it's taking care of your grouchy father, or giving time to volunteer-
ing. . . Duties are obligations that must be fulfilled" (p. 137). The test that
Kant gives for deciding the appropriateness to do or act draws from the
categorical imperatives of telling the truth, keeping promises, and protecting
one's own life. It follows that some of the basic duties for the specific case of
the African Diaspora and their home leaders should include the following:

- the duty or obligation of always telling the truth
- the duty or obligation of always keeping your promises
- the duty and obligation of never committing suicide

As it stands, that African leaders must abide by the duty of ensuring free and
open elections to their Diaspora appears overall as a categorical obligation or
duty that ought to be fulfilled. On the other hand, it is noteworthy that for the
African Diaspora, voting in home countries does not amount to a categorical
duty or universal obligation as Kant conceived it. He draws a line between
ethical obligations, that is, those that derive from juridical or legal duty and
ethical duty. The former obligations come with external constraints which
entail legal consequences while the latter—ethical duty—constitutes a must-
do given that it reasonably fulfills one's beliefs about what one ought to act
upon. For example, voting between the age of eighteen and seventy is legally
compulsory in Brazil (Power, 2006). Consider two Brazilians in this age
range who cast their ballots. The first Brazilian national might do so believ-
ing that it is an ethical duty (I ought to respect the law of the country that

obligates me to vote), whereas the second Brazilian fulfills the legal obligation to vote for fear of being fined. According to Kant's thinking, the Brazilian with ethical belief (as opposed to legal intent) is more likely to cast a ballot in the country's elections. Kant separates ethical arguments from legal arguments by maintaining that the former is what we ought to do all the time. According to him, ethical duty is not an external rule (such as the obligation to vote in Brazil) that is imposed upon the people; rather it is something people consider as inherently good. However, echoing Kantian distinction between moral/ethical and legal duties, the emeritus bishop of Lubango in Angola, Don Zacarias Kamwenho, elevates the duty to vote to an ethical obligation. In fact, voting is not a legally binding obligation in that country. The bishop urged people to consider voting as a moral/ethical obligation, and to participate in the recent election of August 31, 2012. He considered that a citizen's participation in the national precincts constitutes a moral obligation entailing a civic and democratic duty for the achievement of and consolidation of peace and national reconstruction.

Besides the categorical imperatives deemed not negotiable, Kant also admitted that some duties don't stand the test of absoluteness since they can be stated as hypothetical commands, therefore becoming *hypothetical imperatives*. While unconditional commands must be obeyed at all times by all men and women, including African leaders and their Diaspora, hypothetical commands can be stated with an "if" form because they only apply if one wants a certain result. Kant contends that our hypothetical imperatives come from our desires and are conditioned by our interest to act or do something. Examples of hypothetical imperatives might include:

- if you want to vote in Angolan national elections, then you should become an Angolan citizen
- if you have some financial fortune, then invest in the development of your home country in the Global South
- if you are offered a secure job in a home country, then you can return to work in your country of birth

Kant's categorical and hypothetical imperatives sum up in ethical obligations. Ruggiero (2008) states that "every significant human action occurs, directly or indirectly, in a context of relationships with others. And relationships usually imply obligations; that is restrictions on our behavior, demands to do something or to avoid doing it." In his book, *Thinking Critically about Ethical Issues*, Ruggiero (2008) distinguishes three basic criteria for judging the morality of an action, that is, obligations, moral ideals, and consequences. He maintains that obligations come as a consequence of our human relationships and can be divided into obligations of friendship, formal agreement, and obligations of citizenship. While such an obligation of friendship as keeping confidence is worth considering, the other obligations (formal agreement and obligation of citizenship) are more relevant to the ethical dilemma of whether African Diaspora ought to vote in their home countries. Taking the oath of office as president, governor, or leader of a polity stands for the highest form of agreement or formal obligation. Whenever a leading figure enters into a similar contract, be it with a population or an institution, we consider the leader ethically bound to live up to his or her oath of office.

However, obligations might clash with each other. The question of whether African Diaspora should participate in political elections raises the issues of duty-based and desire-based ethics. First, does African Diaspora hold any political right whatsoever in their birth countries? Or does their financial contribution in the form of remittances grant them automatic rights to voting in those countries? Second, what are the consequences of the Diaspora elections on the social, economic, and political wellness of their countries?

The question of African Diasporans' suffrage entails a minimum of two decipherable conflicts of obligations, the obligation of citizenship versus the duty to ensure fair, honest and transparent elections. The same obligation of citizenship collides with the obligation of paying taxes, raising the issue of honesty toward the larger citizenry. Ruggiero states "Obligations of citizenship in democracy demand concern for the conduct of government and responsible participation in the electoral process" (Ruggiero, p.80). The caveat is that those political obligations are not automatically extended to those who have left their countries of origin for various reasons. As the BBC survey has shown, some African Diaspora members have rejected the duty to vote in their home countries whether or not the electoral law of those countries allow them such participation. However, the point in discussion is less of whether the African Diaspora abide by their obligation to elect political leaders in their home countries than whether they ought to bear the right to vote by virtue of their belonging to a country's citizenry. One thing is the voluntary refusal to take part in the voting process in one's country, which constitutes a deontological failure; the other is the denial of entitlement resulting to the disenfranchisement of a group of voters. For Davis (2011) who equates deontology to obedience to laws, "it is our compliance with the law, and that alone, that establishes us as persons of rectitude" (p. 217), relinquishment of the right to vote—assuming voting was a legal obligation like in Brazil—amounts to an ethical infringement. Although I acknowledge the existence of some unethical laws, the point of concern in this section of the book regards the great portion of the African Diaspora, which believes in an innate (human) or constitutional right to vote in their home country. This African Diaspora can be divided into two critically important groups of those that hold a dual citizenship and the rest that have kept loyalty to their sole country of birth. Equating these two groups as far as the right to elect leaders in their home country would amount to an ethical stretch. First, I will consider the case of dual citizenship.

DIASPORA IN DUAL CITIZENSHIP

At this point of my discussing duty-based leadership ethics, it pays to remind the distinction between African "dual nationality" and "dual citizenship." Although both terms are often taken interchangeably to mean nationals of a given state or country, a technical difference is worth mentioning to delineate the scope of this study. A national stands for an individual human that holds a legal relationship with the nation state. The state confers some legal protection to the national while the national holds some obligations toward the state. A person with nationality in a country or state is considered a member of the particular state with limited rights. Yet, an individual with citizenship holds all the legal and political rights and responsibilities due to citizens of a given state. Jones-Correa (2001) specifies that while a person with dual citizenship can vote in any of his or her two countries, an individual with nationality cannot legally be entitled to elections rights. My ethical analysis is concerned with the right to election as I begin discussing duty ethics in the context of dual citizenship.

Advocating for a dual citizenship for the African Diaspora, Archer (2008) ties his arguments to an implicit natural right for "*all* persons of African descent to return to their respective ancestral homelands as citizens, while maintaining their current citizenship status" (p.1). Although Archer's primary rationale for a dual citizenship lies on the overall support citizens living abroad, including African Americans, procure to the African continent's economy, he also believes that a dual citizenship constitutes an answer to those in the Diaspora who psychologically long for a connection to home. Archer sees some sort of umbilical relationship between holders of an African passport and a legal obligation toward the homeland, though such an obligation is not clearly extended to the right to vote in the country of origin. Archer's is a plea to most African countries whose Diaspora appear to be embroiled in an ethical conflict of obligations, mainly that of loyalty to the homeland against the obligation of loyalty to the country of residence. As Shain & Wittes (2002) affirm, the African Diaspora can face a serious clash of loyalties, particularly when a conflict of interest arises between their homeland and their host state. Scholars hold it that when torn between these two loyalties, the majority of the Diaspora is likely to favor their homeland at the detriment of their host countries. In effect, a study by Staton, Jackson, and Canache (2007) concluded that dual citizens do not easily assimilate with the culture and politics of their host countries. The numbers below reflect the low level of loyalty people of Latin America hold toward the

United States: thirty-two percent less likely to be fluent in English; eighteen percent less likely to identify as "American"; nineteen percent less likely to consider the United States as their homeland; eighteen percent less likely to express high levels of civic duty; nine percent less likely to register to vote; fifteen percent less likely to have ever voted in a national election. Loyalty to homeland is determined by various activities the Diaspora exercise throughout the world on its behalf, such as working for the national interest of homeland, support for elected political leaders, and lobbying for homeland's interests. For most members of the African Diaspora, and even for the homeland leaderships, working for the benefits of one's country of birth accounts for a filial duty towards the motherland.

Anupam Chander's (2001) contribution to the question of dual citizenship and citizen loyalty is worth considering insofar as it might constitute an example of an ethical compromise in this regard. In his article "Diaspora Bonds," he calls for a hybrid model of citizenship and loyalty he identifies as the "diaspora model." Said Chander, evidence has it that we live in a globalized world that requires a new paradigm of relations between states and people in the Diaspora. He proposes that members of the Diaspora be allowed to construct their own national and transnational communities according to which "one's loyalty can be to the country in which one lives, the country or countries from which one's ancestors came, the diaspora to which one belongs, or all or none of the above" (p. 1008). His model calls for the Diaspora to be able to live and thrive with dual and overlapping loyalties and sovereigns. Chander's solution to the question of loyalty due to dual citizenship amounts to the following compromise: in the matters of public concern, the member of Diaspora ought to respect the sovereignty of the adopted country; in the matters of private disputes, Diaspora members would choose to respect the laws of their homeland. To my knowledge, no legislation has embraced or moved forward the ethics behind Chander's hybrid "diaspora model" of dual citizenship. Nonetheless, in most instances, this loyalty to either country and filial duty to homeland is not paired with a right to elect the leadership of the homeland. Constitutionally speaking, the majority of African countries including the D.R. Congo, Ghana, and Zimbabwe prohibit dual citizenship (Tungwarara, 2007). Diaspora members must forfeit their political rights, including the right to vote and be voted for, in their homeland when deciding to adopt a second country. According to Archer (2008), countries that do not support the African dual citizenship concept argue that the very status of bearing two national identities would sooner or later end up in conflicting "loyalties" in such instances as war. Yet to many African leaders, dual citizenship is likely to create significant changes to the culture (practices and beliefs) of the remaining citizens of the country/region. Furthermore, it is argued that legally speaking, dual citizenship might bring about serious conflicts as far as issues of taxation; civil status, inheritance, and the like are concerned. Sood (2012) adds another disadvantage to the members of the Diaspora seeking a dual citizenship. As dual citizens, they may have to pay taxes and/or register for military service in their adopted countries. The author gives the example of the Global South country of South Korea that allows dual citizenship until the age of twenty-one, and demands that men eighteen years of age and above complete military service. Although the military service requirement seems not to exist throughout Africa as a precondition for potential dual citizenship, the question of paying taxes is alive in some countries such as Zimbabwe. Zimbabwe, however, seems to follow suit the legal requirements in such countries as the United States and Canada to which their citizens, no matter their current of residence, must pay taxes on their earnings.

In the contrary, some U.S. citizens of Ghanaian descent hold that "one of the benefits of dual citizenship is the ability of dual citizens to influence economic and political decisions in our respective host countries in favor of Ghana, our country of descent" (Maame Ama Djaba, 2009). The author said that Ghana Citizen Advocacy Group, a Ghanaian Diaspora organization contributed 1 billion dollar to its economy in 2009. The group is advocating for the change of the Constitution to allow dual citizens full political rights, entailing the obligation to vote. Sood (2012) reports that many countries have found ways to draw benefits from dual citizenship; Italy used dual nationality as a means to curtail its population decline in the 1990s. Currently, said Sood, birthright citizenship can be granted to anyone whose parent, grandfather, or great-grandfather bore Italian citizenship. However, with an average population growth of two percent per year, African countries might not subscribe to a dual citizenship policy in order to boost up their demography. Another interesting case is that of Dominica and St. Kitts and Nevis, two Global South nations from the Caribbean that hold "economic citizenship programs," which consists of selling citizenships without a requirement for residency. This program is similar to the policy in use in the Dominican Republic where foreigners can obtain citizenship after residing a minimum of six months in the country and upon an investment in real estate or local businesses.

In 2010, [Re]Brand Africa (2010), a blog dedicated to telling African stories, reported on the meeting of twelve presidents of African nations in Nigeria in 2006 to consider granting dual citizenship to African Americans. The rationale for granting African Americans African citizenships was based upon two main premises. The first premise of what I call "deontological nature" stated that all members of the African Diaspora are by their origin children of the African continent. Therefore, allowing them a dual citizenship in Africa will help them gain a better sense of cultural identity; the move will heal the wounds of separation from Africa; it will give an opportunity for networking and collaboration. Ruggiero (2008) would posit that if African countries recognize African Americans as their own, those countries ought to fulfill their obligations, including that of granting the rights due to citizens, to these valuable sons and daughters who were uprooted by the evil forces of history. On the other hand, African Americans' African citizenship will obligate them to promote the well-being of the continent or their African country of adoption and fellow citizens "by observing the law and respecting the legitimate initiatives of the country's leaders. . . In democracy, it also requires participation in the electoral process. When the country is unjustly attacked, it is also a citizen's responsibility, conscience permitting, to support the country's response. . ." (Ruggiero, p. 97). To my knowledge, the obligations of citizenship as defined, in particular those pertaining to the rights to vote and support of the country in the event of an armed attack, are far from being tackled by the concerned countries. However, I can foresee granting dual citizenship to African Americans with limited legal and ethical rights and obligations.

The second premise is more economy driven and ethically egoistic although it might also be considered utilitarian. The proposal of ethical egocentric-utilitarian in nature consisted of granting African Americans dual citizenships through the African Union, African regions, and individual countries on the grounds that they invest in the socio-economic welfare of those impoverished African nations. As a consequence of such an investment, "African Americans, under this plan, would be allowed to travel freely to [Africa], own property, and start businesses . . . In the sense of nation branding, it would make Africans appear warm, friendly, accepting and sympathetic towards the history of African-Americans" ([Re]Brand Africa, 2010). The proposition sounds egocentric for the simple reason that the move of granting African Americans citizenships in Africa was motivated by the potential investments these members of the Diaspora would certainly make in countries that welcome them. However, the end goal of the move— if implemented—is likely to serve the greater numbers of African people who would benefit from the investment made by African Americans. As presented, this proposal although attractive appears to be ethically flawed if the end, that is, rescuing African countries, justifies the means: extending African citizenship to the African American Diaspora. Worse, this proposal targets only African Americans with sufficient financial resources to invest in their motherlands, leaving out those with limited or no economic means to contribute to the development of Africa.

The advent of the DNA test has made it possible for people of African descent to retrace their African roots and, therefore, the countries of origination. Some prominent African Americans have been linked to Cameroon (Chris Rock), Guinea Bissau (Whoopi Goldberg), and Liberia (Oprah). Isaiah Washington's ancestry has been traced back to the Mende people of Sierra Leone. In her article "Called Back to Africa by DNA," Teresa Watanabe (2009) writes that Isaiah Washington recently became a citizen of Sierra Leone and was even inducted a chieftain in a village of that country. He proudly holds a dual citizenship from Sierra Leone and his birth country, the United States. In an altruistic move, Washington contributed a nearly one million dollars to build a school, retrofit a hospital, and restore a historic slave castle on one island. Many other African Americans have actively participated in the re-building of their motherland through similar altruistic actions. Whether they claim and are given citizenships in countries to which the DNA tests are linking them constitutes a topic of ethical and legal consideration by each individual and country involved.

Arguably, Tinga (2009) in her blog proposes that African American seekers of dual citizenship be granted a status similar to that of India's Diaspora. To accommodate Indians who have lived abroad for generations, India has introduced a dual-citizenship-like status that bears more limited advantages than those associated with usual dual citizenship. Coining the expression "Overseas Citizenship of Africa," (OCA) Tinga envisions that such a status will not concede the right to vote or be voted. Rather, it would allow for multiple entries, some limited form of land ownership, and the right to work and visit anytime. Essentially, the OCA status would represent what Bluhm and Heineman (2007) in their book *Ethics and Public Policy* call "prudent pragmatism," or a consensus whereby both African leaders and the African American Diaspora find a mutual benefit. From the deontological point of view, African countries grantors of OCA meet their obligations to recognize their sons and daughters forcibly removed from them by history. From the egoistic-utilitarian perspectives, African leaders would likely profit from the investment in their countries they have been seeking from African Americans. Lastly, from the altruistic perspective, the African American Diaspora will recover the legitimacy to rescue their brothers and sisters in the mainland of Africa.

I concede that the question of dual citizenship I just touched on remains very complex, particularly because there seems to be no international laws to uphold it, each country and region dealing with the issue as best as it can. To move away from the intricacy of the dual citizenship question, I have opted to include in this book all members of the African Diaspora, regardless of their immigration status, who are recognized as so by their countries of origin. However, if so many countries in Africa exclude those citizens living abroad on the grounds of two nationalities, one would infer that the rest of the bulk of the Diaspora at voting age would automatically take part in the suffrage of their home countries. Nonetheless, the case is far from being true as members of the African Diaspora have been indistinguishably cast away from homeland elections. Arguably the deontological-like argument in favor of enfranchising the Diaspora for elections would go as follows: Every citizen has the right to participate in the economic and political building of their country. Whenever citizens have economic and political duties, they should hold corresponding rights (or obligations). The Diaspora constitutes a citizen body that holds the duty to contribute to the economic development of the country. Therefore, the Diaspora ought to exert its right to political actions, such as participation in elections.

ECONOMIC DUTY VERSUS ELECTION RIGHTS

Does the ethical obligation to participate in the development of home countries procure automatically the right to vote in those countries? On the other hand, does the right to vote in a given country call for the obligation to pay taxes in that country? These questions raise some ethical conflicts that are worth examining in this section. Countries that do not allow full election rights to their citizens living abroad may be torn between their maternal duty to receive remittances from their children abroad and the obligation of justice to grant those children what is considered as their right to vote. The conflict of political maternal duty and election right is well stated by this member of the Ugandan Diaspora: "They [Ugandan political leaders] are interested in the money that we can remit back home, the money that we can send back home. But they do not want to put . . . for us to vote . . . They want the money, they want the support but they do not take our views seriously because we are not there physically to influence the outcome of the election" (Student Interviews, p. 24).

Even in the event that African countries might fulfill the obligation of granting their expats the right to vote, this obligation of justice might also clash against the obligation of fairness to ensure transparent and fair elections in the country. Note that many countries have argued that their limited infrastructure precludes a proper monitoring of the external suffrage. On the Diaspora side, there appears to be a conflict between their obligations (to remittances) against the obligation of fairness as far as tax payment and voting process are concerned. Filial obligation might refer here to the ethical responsibility of members of the African Diaspora to actively get involved in bettering social conditions in their motherlands. In fact, the AU expresses this obligation in ways of expectations when it calls to its children living abroad to join hands in the social economic welfare of the continent. The majority of Africans living in their respective countries have joined their voices to the few members of the Diaspora that see an ethical conflict of the obligations the expats owe to both the political leadership and the economic welfare of their home countries. The economic argument according to which the Diaspora's remittances should or might earn stakeholders political rights in their home countries, including the right to suffrage, appears to be ethically unsustainable. Although one would acknowledge the tremendous impact of that contribution, which amounted to $10.8 billion in 2007, the primary intention of remittances has never been the development of the country as a whole (Ratha & Xu, 2008). Remittances, in the form of gifts, medical supplies, or cash are first of all directed to family or personal purposes. In fact, they might contribute to widen the national gap between haves and have-nots, because only those well-offs with family members in the Western world would benefit from those financial and in-kind gifts. Nnaemeka (2007) writes, "Remittances by Africans in the Diaspora have frequently been cited as a good trade off. But the remittances can hardly make up for the serious consequences of the increasing inequality and the disappearing of the middle class in many developing countries" (p. 135). Aggregated dollars in terms of remittances can also create regional inequalities in such countries as Nigeria and Ghana given that few people from the northern regions of both countries stay overseas. Davis argues that: "Deontologists believe that the right is not to be defined in terms of the good, and they reject the idea that the good is prior to the right. In fact, they believe that there is no clear specifiable relation between doing right and doing good" (p. 206). Davis cites Fried (1978) who specified that the goodness of the ultimate consequences does not guarantee the rightness of the actions which produce them. The two realms are not only distinct for the deontologist, but the right is prior to the good (p. 206). Explicitly, the multifaceted contributions of the African Diaspora to their home countries do not ipso facto constitute a right to vote in their home countries. Such a right should be established and claimed independently of whether or not African expatriates are generous to their countries of birth. The next section will examine some foundations of the "rights to vote" in homelands, which many advocates of external votes have put forward.

Kant's duty-based ethics argues that rules about the treatment of other rational agents must always be followed, "regardless of the consequences" (Morgan, Peach & Mazzucelli, 2004, p. 49). However, there are hardly international rules and regulations in support of the election rights of the Diaspora in their countries of origin. The argument in favor of voting as a birthright is mainly supported by "different international declarations in which universal, equal, free and secret suffrage is recognized as an inalienable part of human rights (for example, the 1948 Universal Declaration of Human Rights, Article 21; the 1948 American Declaration of Human Rights and Duties, Article 20; and the 1969 American Convention on Human Rights, Article 23)" ACE (2010a). These documents do not mention external voting as an integral part of universal suffrage. Nonetheless, the ACE quotes the International Convention on the Protection of the Rights of All Migrant Workers, promulgated in 1990, which explicitly states that: "Migrant workers and members of their families shall have the right to participate in public affairs of their state of origin and to vote and to be elected at elections of that state, in accordance with its legislation. The States concerned shall, as appropriate and in accordance with their legislation, facilitate the exercise of these rights" (ACE, 2010a).

As stipulated above, migrant workers' rights to election would fall in the area of Kantian hypothetical imperative in that such a right is somehow abiding "if" it is in accordance with the legislation of the state of origin. In other words, the Diaspora can only participate in external elections if their home countries deem it appropriate and feasible. The rights of the Diaspora elections should have responded to Kant's norms of categorical imperative if the external voting were an action to be taken always and everywhere and therefore universally applicable. MacIntyre (1966) emphasizes that "categorical imperative is a moral rule without exceptions, and we are not to be concerned with the possible unintended consequences of such application" (p. 194).

ACE underlines the fact that the Diaspora voting as part of universal suffrage is marred by insufficient self-evidence and it remains problematic. One of the classic requirements for voting rights appears to be "residence inside the state territory," which is hardly fulfilled by the majority of expatriates for various reasons, ranging from political to economic affordability. Secondly, by claiming the rights to election in home countries, the Diaspora ought to abide by the obligation of a free and uncorrupt electoral process. However, as many African countries have reported, "the implementation of external voting involves major technical and administrative problems that might interfere with other crucial features of the franchise, in particular the principle of free elections" (ACE 2010a). The rationale for the nebulosity around the current lack of universal understanding and application of external voting might be due to the following factor. Political elites seem very foreign as far as the normative rationale in favor of or against the Diaspora voting is concerned. As a consequence they do not consider the potential problems that may surface were such Diaspora voting rights to be implemented. ARCIE concedes that a great demand of expertise on the Diaspora voting is paramount; so are the options for its institutionalization. The below examples underscore the newness of this topic as well as the "chaotic" quest by individual countries for the foundation and implementation of leadership ethics as they engage the question of the African Diaspora voting. Although Angola is listed as a country with external elections for its Diaspora, no Angolans living abroad were allowed to vote in the recent elections of August 2012. To the question of "Can a voter who resides abroad cast a ballot in the national election?" the International Foundation for the Electoral System (2012) reported as follows:

> Under Article 143 in the Constitution, Angolan citizens who are residing abroad for the purposes of work, study, illness or a similar reason may vote in

national elections. However, the national election commission has not been able to implement the logistics of diaspora voting, whether in Angolan Embassies or Consulates around the world or elsewhere. The election commission also cancelled the early voting for members of the military, police, firemen and election observers who will be at work on August 31.

As South Sudanese voted in a referendum on whether to create their own country separate from the North, Karimi (2011) wrote that about 55,000 members of the Southern Sudanese Diaspora casted their ballots in United States and several other countries. Karimi also reports the case of Chol, one of the so-called Lost Boys, who cast his vote from abroad on the South Sudanese referendum. The Sudanese Lost Boys refers to the groups of over 20,000 boys mainly from the current South Sudan who were either displaced or made orphans during the second Sudanese Civil War between 1983 and 2005. Chol is one of the 4,000 Lost Boys now in their twenties and thirties that were resettled in the United States, and have spent the last decade rebuilding their lives. After they escaped the war in Sudan, Chol and his group trekked across deserts and swamps for hundreds of miles and settled as refugees in neighboring countries, living in sprawling camps for years. Chol received the advent of election on the referendum as a dream come true, as he explained: "It's time for them to hear our voices, for us to revolt against all the pain we suffered," the graduate student says. "A lot of people have died for this day. . . I don't care what government comes after this. No government will be worse than what we have. Passing this referendum means my father did not die in vain. It means our children will not live scared lives. . . . We will be the last 'lost boys' Sudan will ever see" (Karimi, 2011).

Leadership ethics appears to be well served in this case of South Sudan, where the obligations of the future citizens meet those of its future state. Chol had been looking forward to fulfilling his duty as a son of South Sudan to engage in the selection of his country's leadership. Besides any cultural, personal, and political motivations, which he obviously holds as a consequence of his painful experience of a Lost Boy, Chol's action of voting amounts to what the Catholic bishop of Angola, the Most Reverend Zacarias Kamwenho, above elevated to the level of "moral obligation."

That the then future South Sudan sought the votes of its "citizens" abroad struck a chord about duty ethics. This future country took the positive side of the hypothetical imperative of Kant in that it paved the way to free and unbiased elections by setting up the minimum administrative infrastructure required for their Diaspora to participate in the elections. What is even more remarkable is the reminder that in spite of its quasi-inexistent socio-development infrastructure, South Sudan, which is the size of Texas but has only thirty miles of paved roads and coming out of two brutal civil wars, has shown ethical leadership as far as the expatriate votes are concerned. One would only hope that now that South Sudan has become its own country, it will continue to abide by deontological ethics, giving their rights to vote to its citizens living abroad.

In 2004, the new South Africa, liberated from the yoke of the apartheid system, rallied all its citizens abroad to vote in the very first democratic elections in the history of that country. The experience was successfully replicated in the 2009 general election. In fact government spokesperson Themba Maseko stated that a significant amount of over 16,000 South Africans living abroad had voted at SA embassies throughout the world (SouthAfrica.Info, 2009). Using a deontological-like argument to explain South African holding of the expatriate elections, Maseko explained that "[South Africans] abroad had strengthened their bonds with their compatriots at home and given substance to the Constitutional Court ruling that South Africans abroad had the right to vote." He reports on the expats' enthusiasm to vote, which recalls that of the South Sudanese Chol. Duty-based ethics would acknowledge the fulfillment of two obligations: that of the citizens of South Sudan and South Africa toward their countries of origin and the obligation of those countries towards their citizens abroad.

Duty-based ethics requires that African states fulfill their obligation to enforce the constitutional rights of their citizens who are migrant workers in other countries. Besides, different African Diasporas have brought political pressure on their "home" government to change the rules on dual citizenship and external elections (Manby, 2009). For example, the Zimbabwean Diaspora in Britain contended that "the exclusion from voting of those living outside Zimbabwe curtailed their rights to freedom of expression to an extent that was not acceptable in democratic society" (Tungwarara, 2007, p. 57). They supported their arguments with clauses from the Universal Declaration of Human Rights, the African Charter on Human and Peoples' Rights, and the Southern African Development Community (SADC) Principles and Guidelines Governing Democratic Elections.

Deontological arguments have been used also to deny the African Diaspora the rights to external voting. In the specific case of Zimbabwe, the government argued that "the electoral law provided for the disqualification of voters who have been absent from Zimbabwe for twelve months or more" (Tungwarara, 2007, p. 58). The argument furthered that the SADC Principles and Guidelines are merely a political and non-binding document paving the ways to democracy. The Zimbabwean government also contended that it was unable to allow electors from the Diaspora to cast their votes because of logistical problems. Most African governments advanced similar duty-based arguments to deny their citizens living abroad their "constitutional" right to voting. Underscored here is the question of a rights-based approach to the electoral administration and how far governments should be held accountable for not implementing Diasporans' right to vote (Bongila 2012). In examining the question of whether the African Diaspora can vote in their countries of origin, this chapter closely holds on to Kant's belief that moral action ought to be done out of a sense of duty rather than by following one's desires (Enomoto & Kramer, 2007). Two categories of duty appeared obvious to me: first that of the home country to ensure that the constitutional obligation—if any—toward the elections of its Diaspora is met. While a handful of African countries, such as South Africa and Angola, include some sort of expatriate voting legislation, most countries either don't have such legal obligation or do not act on it. The second obligation is that of the African Diaspora, many of them have considered their participation in their country elections not as a privilege, but rather a moral duty toward their country of birth. However, most members of the Diaspora see voting as either a human or a constitutional right. This question of the legitimization of the suffrage rights for African expats appears far from being obvious or resolved within the scope of this book, particularly because of the nebulosity surrounding the interpretation of those rights evoked by the Diaspora. In demanding their participation in their countries' elections, the Diaspora rather puts forward utilitarian arguments that are mostly encapsulated in the socio-economic services they render to the polity of their birthplaces. The next chapter is an attempt to analyze the Diaspora "rights to elections" in the lens of utilitarianism.

Chapter Four

African Diaspora Vote in Utility Ethics

Sages have argued: your heart might belong to two countries,
Although you find yourself living in one,
Whether by choice or by life vicissitudes
However, is your heart big enough to hold both?

Whether the African Diaspora holds the right to vote in their birth countries will be discussed in this chapter using the ethical standard referred to as utilitarianism or consequentialism. Utilitarianism finds its roots in the philosophy of a Greek thinker Epicurus (342–270 BCE) for whom "pleasure is a goal that nature has ordained for us; it is also the standard by which we judge every-thing good." This view would hold that the rightness and wrongness of African Diaspora's suffrage in their home countries should be determined by the pleasure or pain such suffrage would produce. The same ethical principle was rendered by Francis Hucheson (1694–1746) for whom an action is best "which procures the greatest happiness to the greatest numbers." In its classical version, this ethical standard has been mainly attributed to Jeremy Bentham and John Stuart Mill. Bentham articulated the two main tenets of utilitarianism, which are teleology or consequentialism and utility or hedonism. According to the consequentialism principle, "the rightness or wrongness of an act is determined by the goodness or badness of the results that flow from it" (Pojman & Fieser: 2012, p. 103). John Stuart Mill's major contribution to this ethical standard is the distinction he established between happiness and mere sensual pleasure, coming up with a version of the principle often referred to as utilitarianism.

Ethically speaking, utilitarianism is a moral theory that treats pleasure or happiness as the only absolute moral good. According to utilitarian thinkers, the morality of your actions depends on their results. Acts that bring about an overall increase in happiness or pleasure are morally good; those that result in suffering or pain are morally bad (Ingram & Parks, p. 149).

In the survey conducted by the BBC, over a third of the respondents argued against the Diaspora's prerogative to voting in their home countries while about sixty-six percent evoked social and economic reasons to make the case for external voting. The respondents' opinions, though not necessarily representative of the whole African Diaspora, provide a stepping-stone for an analysis of leadership ethics based on consequentialism or utilitarianism.

AFRICAN DIASPORA AGAINST VOTE RIGHTS

From the utilitarian standpoint, Diaspora residents standing against the right to vote in their motherland base their arguments on the consequences of such a right of suffrage on the greater number of African nationals. The Diaspora's right to election does not procure the greatest good for the greatest number as Global South people would contract extraordinary expenses to satisfy the Diaspora electorate. Money allocated to other public services, such as education and health care would be directed toward Diaspora outreach. The greatest opposition to the Diaspora's rights to elections in their home countries is raised by citizens in respective countries. A few examples from the BBC's survey would make the point. Chi Primus, from Buea, Cameroon, reacted as follows:

> If they [expatriates] don't pay taxes and contribute to the growth of the country, it doesn't make any sense to give them the chance to choose the leaders. People cannot be staying comfortably abroad and deciding how the country should be run. Many countries cannot manage their elections locally, so how will they manage balloting abroad? (BBC News, 2006).

Diaspora residents standing against the right to vote in their motherland base their arguments mainly on the consequences of such political undertaking. "Consequences" are to be understood as "the beneficial or harmful effects that result from an action and affect the people involved" (Ruggiero, 2004: p. 81). One respondent to the BBC's survey intriguingly stated the following:

> I am a Ugandan living in UK and I do travel home regularly and send money home. However, I don't think Ugandans abroad should be allowed to vote because how would politicians in Uganda campaign in the diaspora? It would mean they would have to travel across the world which could be very expensive. With the current percentage-based voting system where a few votes could change the result, politicians would use this as an excuse to waste government money to travel abroad to campaign (BBC News, 2006: p. 1).

A member of the Somalia Diaspora of the Twin Cities, Minnesota, echoes the above concern when he agrees with the statement by the prime minister of Algeria whom he quoted as saying to the Diaspora: "You guys did not take part in the problem of the country, you were not here; you escaped; you really were not part of us for this long. To come back and say: we will help you rebuild the country . . . do you really know enough about our problems? Do you really know any more about our country?" (Student Interviews, 2011, p. 60). Bazeyi Hategekimana, a U.S. resident, sharply reacted in these terms: "We African Diasporas are seeking our own success, getting permanent residence papers or citizenship in Western countries. Africans abroad represent a small population of the whole continent and their vote can't have an impact. The continent needs many things and most of them are more important than casting a ballot" (BBC News, 2006).

The above statements closely relate to Jeremy Bentham's (1748–1833) utilitarianism, which holds that the goodness of an act must be measured by its consequences in society, which should be calculated as pleasures and pains (Bluhm and Heineman, 2007). Bentham equated social good with the greatest good of the greatest number. The consequences of the African Diaspora's election would likely reflect negatively on the already challenged economies of their Global South countries for two major reasons. First governments would overstretch their budget to track down the number of eligible electors throughout the world. They would be pressured to secure absentee ballots, and use expensive means to disseminate them to different corners of the globe in order to reach out to their Diasporas. Secondly politicians and particularly campaigners would certainly utilize public money that could have been allocated to education, health care and the like to reach out to the Diaspora.

The utilitarianism or desire-based argument against the Diaspora's election might go as follows: the Diaspora's right to election does not procure the greatest good for the greatest number. Global South people would contract extraordinary expenses to satisfy the Diaspora electorate. Money allocated to other public services, such as education and health care, would be directed toward Diaspora outreach. The Diaspora's right to election is likely to have negative effects on the economies of Global South countries of Africa and its people.

AFRICAN DIASPORA FOR VOTE RIGHTS

A desire-based rationale might above all justify a pro-Diaspora's suffrage premise. Although rebuked by its opponents, the major argument raised by the proponents of the Diaspora's right to suffrage is highly economic as restated by Mabinda from Munich, Germany: "Since we actively contribute to the GDP of our home countries, it should be obvious that we also take part in elections. Ugandans in the Diaspora send more money home than Uganda earns from her exports. Therefore we should have a say in who is supposed to run that country. Some of those at home living on our hard cash should stop insulting us" (BBC News, 2006). Like Mabinda, those in favor of voting rights for the Diaspora argue that the political exercise of voting will contribute to nation building, and to designing a true "respublica" and a true government that will benefit the greatest population. It promotes a more efficient government that works for the benefit of all; it is likely to supply government and decision makers with better information; it will allow citizens to obey laws consciously and voluntarily; it will increase social and individual benefits; it will enhance people's perception of their own effectiveness and responsibility in their own life and that of others. The African Governance Monitoring and Advocacy Project (AfriMAP)[1] stated that "Elections are at the heart of democratic political participation" (AfriMAP, 2009, p. 8), and Mozambican leadership provides an example of a state that extended the voting right to its Diaspora to unify the former war-torn country in a democratic process. Writing about the leadership of South Africa and its effort to secure the Diaspora's vote in 1994, AfriMAP (2006) lays out some positive impacts of such a deliberative or participatory democracy. It promotes more efficient government that works for the benefit of all; it is likely to supply government and decision makers with better information; it will allow citizens to obey laws consciously and voluntarily; it will increase social and individual benefits; it will enhance people's perception of their own effectiveness and responsibility in their own life and that of others. Political participation of all, including the Diaspora's, has increased in South Africa since the inception of full democracy in 1994: "more black people share the privileges and the access to power and wealth that used to be restricted to white South Africans" (AfriMAP, 2006, p. 27).

The antithetic argument that most members of the African Diaspora had abandoned their home country to its own fate, and therefore, cannot attempt to influence its current political matters often finds the following rebuttal from the expatriates: "Listen, we took part in helping to sustain your lives; we did not comfortably live in our host-countries . . . because our minds were always with you (our home-country fellows), and our wealth was always coming to you, we were sending money; we really did not have time to save up anything" (Student Interviews, p. 60). Grace Okeng (BBC News, 2006) explains: "Working and living abroad does not strip one of their citizenship and the right to participate in national governance. In any case Africans living abroad remit a lot of money back to their countries to support their economies. It is therefore unreasonable to deny them the right to decide who should be entrusted with the governance of their countries. As a Ugandan I feel cheated that I won't be going to the polls."

In her article "Development Challenges for a Resurgent African Diaspora," Davies (2010) expands on African governments' move to tap the Diaspora for a greater participation in the socio-economic welfare of their home countries. Among various development initiatives taken by the Diaspora, the author cites the following: "non-government organizations (NGOs), capital, regional, pan-continental and international organizations" (p. 131). As a consequence, African governments are courting their Diasporas to tap the potential of such flows and networks as safe transfer of remittances, contribution to the Millennium Development Goals (MDGs), and innovative skills to help promote political stability and territorial security. African governments' *telos* to offer the greatest good (social development) to the greatest number of their citizens can only be realized through the Diaspora. This increased cooperation of the African leaders has emboldened most members of Diaspora in their demand for the enhancement of partnerships on many fronts such as formulation of win-win immigration frameworks, but particularly the adoption and/or implementation of external processes to national suffrage. South Africa, for example, has hailed the partnership with its citizens living overseas, which has resulted in greater socio-economic investment in the country. It goes so far as to see a real benefit for the greater number of South African people in the phenomenon of "flight of competences" or brain drain, by turning it into "brain bank."

BRAIN DRAIN AND BRAIN BANK

The erosion of academic and professional competences—brain drain—has also been evoked by the opponents of the Diaspora rights to elections as a social, economic, and intellectual loss by the African society of citizens that could contribute to the development of the continent. In his book *Globalization of Education*, Joel Spring (2009) defines brain drain as the movement of educator and skilled workers from low-income nations and rural centers to more prosperous nations and/or urban centers. While some countries experience brain gain for attracting skilled immigrants, the phenomenon of brain waste occurs when immigrants to more developed countries do not find a job commensurate to their educational qualifications. When educated immigrants return to their countries with their qualification or they become transnational with homes in different countries, Spring (2009) calls this brain circulation. Whatever angle you spin this phenomenon of human capital flight, many African countries holding desire-based ethics views contend that home countries remain the bigger losers. It is estimated that African countries lose 4 billion dollars in the employment of 150,000 Diaspora members annually. The United Nations for Development Programs report that a country such as Ethiopia produces excellent doctors, the majority of whom are found in

Chicago's hospitals rather than in their homeland's. *Ownership, Leadership and Transformation: Can We Do Better for Capacity Development?* by Lopez & Theisohn (2003) provides a more comprehensive analysis of the brain-drain phenomenon worldwide. Often cited are the examples of Ghana and South Africa to illustrate this rather less optimistic utilitarian view of the so-called "brain drain."

Ghana, for example has suffered severe consequences of the drain of its doctors and nurses by developed countries. Ghana has an estimated 3,600 doctors, one for every 6,700 inhabitants, compared to one doctor per 430 people in the United States (The World Bank, 2011). However, Ghana's doctors and nurses leave their homeland for better conditions of life in the United States, England, and Canada. Another example often cited is that of South Africa, which has reportedly been experiencing a brain drain for the last two decades. This human exodus is seen as a negative factor for the well-being of the poor in the southern African region, which has to rely on health care facilities particularly in its effort to curtail the prevalence of the HIV/AIDS epidemic. The ethical consequences of South Africa brain drain amounts to a potential damage to the regional economy, and a national economic imbalance given that more White than Black expertise is migrating abroad. To limit the social-economic erosion, Amy Jo Ehman and Patrick Sullivan (2001) report that South Africa demanded in 2001 that Canada stop the recruitment of doctors and highly skilled medical personnel from South Africa. It has been estimated that South Africa has incurred about 1.41 billion dollars of loss on returns from the investment for its emigrating doctors. Meanwhile the gain for developed countries where those skilled workers have landed has been estimated at 2.7 billion dollars for the United Kingdom alone (Mills et al., 2011).

Thus, the utilitarian argument against brain drain would go as follows: African countries lose skilled workers, such as doctors, engineers, and others to developed countries. By attracting African skilled workers, such developed countries as the United States, Canada, and Britain benefit from the expertise that should have been used in home countries. Because of brain drain, underdeveloped countries are losing the little expertise they must count on to better the social-economic conditions of their impoverished people. Therefore, brain drain is detrimental to the greater number of African populations that rely on their own for better economic outlooks.

As opposed to the brain drain viewpoint, some African leaders and scholars have put forward the concept of "brain bank." Expressing his enthusiasm at the massive participation of the South African Diaspora in the general elections of 2009, government spokesperson Themba Maseko stated that the eagerness of the South African expatriates who voted abroad in the general elections could be seen as a "brain bank" for the country. For him South Africans living abroad are likely to improve the country's image abroad in addition to bringing investment, knowledge, and skills back into their motherland. The design of this brain bank has caused South Africa to put forth some organizations, such as the Homecoming Revolution, and the International Marketing Council's Global South Africans network, to enhance the connections between South Africans living abroad and their home country (BuaNews, 2009). Desire-based ethicist views on the Somalians living in the Twin Cities, Minnesota, where they form the largest agglomeration besides Mogadishu, would likely be that of the brain drain factor. However, interviewed on how he perceived himself as an educated Somali living in the Twin Cities, Minnesota, this student sees himself as a component of the Somali brain bank or brain circulation.

> As far as my "Americaness," I consider I'm as American as apple pie. For me, if Somalia was stable, if Somalia was at peace, if Somalia did not need me, I would not be involved. I would be. . . I've settled my life here, I'm happy where I'm at, but unfortunately, when you have part of your body burning, you concentrate on that part. That part now is visible and I want to help out. So there's no political loyalty, but loyalty to the country of my birth. I know that you've heard of the term, "brain-drain," because I learned it in the classes that we took together, but have you heard of the term, "circulation"? So that, rather than losing people or losing that resource, it's more of a. . . it's not a "drain" . . . I don't know if I'm explaining myself very well, but the intellectual resource that was lost by people leaving different countries in Africa (and Somalia is one of those), it's somehow being returned (Student Interviews, p. 59).

The closest the African Diaspora can come to a certain suffrage in home countries is to become vocal in their support of elected homeland political leaders. The Diaspora can also express their dismay about certain politicians in their homeland that might be betraying national causes. Kwaku Kyem (n.d.) for example reports that the hands of the Ghanaian members of the Diaspora that feed their relatives in their homeland have an obvious influence on the choices that their kinsmen make in selecting leaders of the country. Kwaku Kyem confirms that Ghanaians in the Diaspora exhibit a remarkable influence on the electoral process at home, holding the ability to stir a popular and spontaneous uprising to demand their participation in Ghanaian elections, if they really felt it suitable.

In an attempt to reclaim their rights to vote in the parliamentary elections, some members of the Zimbabwean Diaspora living in Britain took the country to court in 1995. They argued that they were being punished for leaving the country, whereas their lawyer added that "the denial of citizens resident in a foreign country to vote is not reasonably justifiable in a democratic society" (BBC News, 2005). Zimbabwe's diplomats and military personnel and their families abroad are the only "expatriates" qualified to vote. In 2005,

Zimbabwe's Supreme Court ruled that over three million expatriates from Zimbabwe would not vote. The government of President Mugabe stated that the other expatriates had to return to Zimbabwe if they wished to vote. Alleging accusations of fraud and violence in two previous elections, Zimbabwean justice minister Patrick Chinamasa argued that the expatriates' request for home elections was "far-fetched and virtually impossible" as it would require major changes to the electoral laws (BBC News, 2005).

NOTES

1. "The Africa Governance Monitoring and Advocacy Project (AfriMAP), is a program of the Open Society Foundations and a civil society initiative that aims to promote good governance in Africa. AfriMAP's vision is of democratic, fair and effective governance in African countries and its mission is to influence law, policy, and practice in specific areas for better protection of human rights, improved governance, and strengthened democratic oversight and engagement" (http://www.afrimap.org/board.php).

Chapter Five

African Diaspora Vote in Virtue Ethics

UNDERSTANDING ETHICS OF VIRTUE

A smooth introduction to the virtue theory of ethics and its application to the dilemma posed by the rights to election for the African Diaspora may begin with these two practical examples. Bella is originally from Liberia, but has been working as a registered nurse in the United States for the last twenty years and made a good living. She learns about a Liberian grassroots organization that provides social and education support to over one thousand former child soldiers. At the brink of closing for lack of financial support, the organization is appealing for $100,000 to keep on with its philanthropic mission. Bella is profoundly moved by the appeal, and feeling deep sorry, she sends one hundred dollars to the organization. Angela hears the same news but does not feel any sorrow about the former child soldiers that are being reintegrated in society. However, out of sense of duty for her country of origin, she sends one hundred dollars from her own pocket. The second case concerns Badibanga and Mvumbi, both members of the African Diaspora who were offered two positions as finance minister and director of the Central Bank in their native country of the Democratic Republic of the Congo. Badibanga and Mvumbi had both the opportunity to embezzle 10 million dollars from the public coffers. Badibanga never considers embezzling, and the idea of behaving in a sneaky manner has never crossed his mind. Mvumbi on the other hand struggles with the temptation and almost succumbs to it. However, through an exceptional effort, he succeeds in not putting his hand on the common good.

> Your virtues can become your vices. So the lesson here is: act in moderation. In order to really lead a virtuous life; don't go overboard with any one virtue (Ingram & Parks, 2002, P. 107).

In each of these two cases, the Liberian Bella and the Congolese Badibanga behaved more morally than Angela and Mvumbi because they have internalized their moral convictions by doing the right in a spontaneous manner. They do not have to reflect on their conducts nor do they have to struggle over them. Thus, Bella and Badibanga have virtues, those special qualities or "trained behavioral dispositions that result in habitual acts of moral goodness" (Pojman & Fieser, 2012 p. 146). The antipode of virtue is vice, which amounts to "trained behavioral dispositions that result in habitual acts of moral wrongness" (p. 147). The central premise of virtue ethics holds that the role of morality is to produce excellent persons, who, acting out of the spontaneous goodness of their hearts, serve as examples for other people. Both Bella and Badibanga are morally good persons for the simple reason that their good characters enable them to spontaneously do the right thing.

To the question of what does it mean to be a good person, ethicists have mainly relied upon the thinking of two Greek philosophers, Plato (ca. 428–354 BCE) and Aristotle (ca. 384–322 BCE). For Plato, a virtuous citizen was one who demonstrated good character by fulfilling the citizen's role in the city, regardless of his or her social status (slave or master). Generally speaking, society views those individuals who accumulate a range of virtues and fulfill their roles and responsibilities as being virtuous. Plato offered a short list that has been dubbed cardinal virtues, including wisdom, temperance, courage, and justice. The New Testament has provided three additional virtues, called theological, that are: faith, hope, and charity. Christianity as well as other world religions have all added and preached to the virtues that should make a human excellent or holy.

While Plato believed that for a person to learn to discern ethical virtues, he or she should study mathematics and sciences, his student Aristotle disagreed. For the latter, experience combined with the right beliefs would result in ethical wisdom. In his classic work, *Nicomachean Ethics*, Aristotle called virtues those characteristics that allow people to live well in communities. In order for a community of people to achieve individual welfare, there needs to be proper social institutions such a good government or administration. According to Aristotle, the function of a human ruler (or leader) is to govern society well, and that of the individual is to use reason in pursuit of the good life (in Greek, *eudaimonia*). Ethics, as Aristotle understands it, is an integral part of politics. He distinguishes intellectual virtues from the moral ones. The intellectual virtues may be taught directly whereas the moral ones must be lived to be learned. We acquire the right habits, that is, the virtues by living well. A morally well lived life consists of living in moderation, according to the Golden Mean. Aristotle places virtues at the Golden Mean, that is, the middle ground between excess and deficiency. For example, the virtue of courage stands as the mean between cowardice and foolhardiness, while liberality is the mean between stinginess and unrestrained giving. In the *Nicomachean Ethics*, Aristotle writes:

> We can experience fear, confidence, desire, anger, pity, and generally any kind of pleasure and pain either too much or too little, and in either case not properly. But to experience all this at the right time, toward the right objects, toward the right people, for the right reason, and in the right manner—that is the mean and the best course, the course that is the mark of virtue (Aristotle, 2007, book 2).

To illustrate his point about the Golden Mean, Aristotle stated that a foot soldier with too much courage can become reckless to the point of endangering the lives of fellow soldiers. In the contrary, too little courage, implying fear and hesitancy, can make the foot soldier commit the same mistakes. Thus, Aristotle observed that there is only one right standard of moderation that all humans should be aiming for. Based upon his writing, an ethical leader demonstrates the virtues of courage, temperance, generosity, self-control, honesty, sociability, modesty, fairness, and justice (Northouse, 2010).

In leadership, scholars often see virtue ethics in the guise of trait theory, which is an attempt to describe a charismatic leader as the embodiment of particular traits. Trait theory of leadership is rooted in the premise that a person is born to be a leader or the person is a natural leader. It suggests that certain people or individuals possess special innate or inborn characteristics or abilities that make them leaders, and that those characteristics set them apart from those that are not leaders. Such personal qualities as height, intelligence, extraversion, and fluency are often used to refer to charismatic leaders (Northouse, 2010).

Essentially, virtue-based ethics stems from being and becoming a good and worthy human being. In spite of the truth that people have the ability to learn and develop good values, virtue theory holds that virtues are inherent in one's disposition. Good values or virtues become, therefore, habitual and part of humans when they practice those virtues over time from youth to adulthood. "By telling the truth, people become truthful, by giving to the poor, people become benevolent; by being fair to others, people become just. Our virtues are derived from our actions, and our actions manifest our virtues" (Northouse, p. 382).

VIRTUE OF *KIMUNTU*

African ethics is also concerned with the above list of qualities that depict a good person. Worth mentioning is the African virtue of *ubuntu* or *kimuntu* or *bomoto* (in two Congolese languages), whose meaning is often summarized in this proverbial saying: "I am because we are, and because we are, I am too" (Bujo, 2011, p.5). This foundational principle articulates the conviction that each African becomes a whole human being only in the fellowship of life with other people. Such a humanity-orientation virtue is engrained in the heart of each member of the African Diaspora as they feel bound by the obligation of remitting to their family, their communities, and ultimately their home countries. Ideally, the *kimuntu* principle does not refer exclusively to members of one's own family, clan, or ethnicity although these initial groups constitute the basis for larger relationships. Rather it goes beyond the close family ties to embrace the view that humans act more effectively when they hold fast to solidarity with their like. It, thus, includes participatory compassion and charitable contribution that encompass universal perspectives, hospitality, daily friendships, and dialogue with other members in order to uplift the community and the country as a whole.

Whether we call it *kimuntu* or "communitarianism," the solidarity and love that the African Diaspora holds for their kin and country people still living in their motherland constitutes an essentially fundamental virtue that is deeply engrained in their being. That every single member of the Diaspora provides to friends, siblings, parents, cousins, and mere acquaintances needs only to be underscored. This communal innate disposition is not always easily understood by the Western mentality rooted in an individualistic capitalism. In his book *Foundations of an African Ethic*, Bujo (2011) explains that the African people would strip themselves of their humanity had they behaved without consideration for interpersonal relationships and solidarity with the community. One, however, does not become a leader or a just person because of one's concrete actions or achievements. Rather a Diaspora member remains authentic to his or her being by means of relations. "This means that the human person in Africa is from the very beginning in a network of relationships that constitutes his inalienable dignity" (p. 88). A meaningless portion of the African Diaspora, however, has embraced and adopted the individualistic Western mentality that has led to their losing the essence of *kimuntu*, at least as far as caring for the motherland is concerned, and seen by the rest of the community as selfish and unethical.

Virtue ethics as applied to the context of the right to suffrage of African Diaspora surfaces two categories of rationales. On the one hand, people have denounced the "viciousness" of the expatriates in their claim for participation in their home country's elections. On the other hand, there has been outpouring of support of the "goodness" of the Diaspora related to the morality of their entitlement to their right to vote. I will consider the aforementioned list of cardinal and theological virtues, in addition to "African *kimuntu*," to examine the two schools of thought. One question that comes to mind is why would a Diaspora's demand for the right to elect political leaders in their motherland amount to a vicious action? I will address this rather broad question as it relates adequately to virtue ethics: What virtues or moral ideals are involved when the African Diaspora engages in the process of home-country election? I understand virtues as "aspects of excellence or . . . goals that bring greater harmony in one's self and between self and others" (Ruggiero, 2007, p. 80).

As stated earlier, arguments of the virtue-ethics nature exist evoking the lack of love, compassion, and integrity from the part of the Diaspora in their quest for a birthright to vote in home countries. Those arguments hold that the Diaspora's compassion for their home country seems to have been lost in many regards (Starratt, 2004). Given the African economies already under dire stress, the African Diaspora's claim to election right may also raise the issues of (lack of) compassion, (lack of) fairness, (lack of) care, (lack of) *ubuntu, kimuntu,* or *bomoto,* and (lack of) integrity. One BBC respondent addresses this question: "Citizens who live in the country have the country in heart more than those abroad and they know what is going on better. Their votes have a direct impact on them. Hence no messing up in who to vote for" (BBC News, 2006, p. 2). This quote attributes to the Diaspora the flip side of virtue of compassion, which amounts to a combination of vices like careless-ness and insensitivity. For compassion, from Latin (*cum-pati*) or co-suffer-ing, can be understood as the virtue of empathy for the hurt of others. Re-garded as the basic part of human love and the stepping-stone for greater social interaction, compassion gives rise to an active desire to alleviate the suffering of others. The African virtue of *kimuntu* owes its value to compas-sion because it is the key ingredient of African communitarism and altruism. Compassion, therefore, embodies the ageless golden rule consisting of "*Do to others what you would have them do to you.*" In the revolving discussions of whether ethical virtues bear a contextual or universal value, compassion stands the test of time and space as it crosses every culture and religion.

The argument that the African Diaspora lacks compassion for claiming their rights to elections in home countries is based on that those expatriates seem careless about the misery of the people who live under socio-economic hardships. Instead of contributing their effort to alleviate the economic dur-ess of their home countries, the Diaspora would exacerbate the conditions of underdevelopment for lack of compassion and understanding. It costs extra financial burden, extra infrastructure, and extra manpower to run external votes, and holding those elections will take a toll on social programs, which governments may be funding with the money they would be forced to allo-cate to the external voting were it to be adopted as a national policy. If the Diaspora was really preoccupied by their country-people's socio-economic lack of welfare, they would have their focus set on altruistic remittances instead of stirring up the causes of social harms by ways of elections.

In addition, those citizens living abroad are likely to vote for politicians whose views on major issues pertaining to current social contexts of their home countries might be nebulous or even detrimental for the people. If the candidates would have to campaign abroad as did Ghanaian candidates in 2004, they would certainly depend on the public treasury (Kwasi, 2006). Most people in grassroots Ghana would rather have the health and education systems improved to cut down infantile death and adult illiteracy.

Besides the question of (lack of) compassion, the Diaspora's claim to election rights raises the issue of fairness and integrity. Those opposed to extending the rights of elections to the Diaspora perceive such behavior as not only a lack of fairness but also that of integrity. A person of integrity is highly regarded as displaying reliability, trustworthiness, honesty, and being principled. Ethically speaking, moral integrity is a virtue manifested by a person who can be counted on to behave in way that is constant and harmonious (Ingram & Parks, 2002). Yet opponents of the Diaspora's claims for election rights advance that those critical two virtues of fairness and integrity are absent from the expatriates' registry, at least as far as voting in their home countries is concerned. For example Magaisa (2009) acknowledges that the Diaspora does not pay taxes in Zimbabwe, which has prompted the government to require compliance to this civic duty as a precondition for voting, in addition to having lived one full year within the country. Opponents of the Diaspora's right to election contend that those who don't contribute to the government's public revenues ought not to be granted the same right as most of the poor citizens who use their meager incomes to pay taxes for the public good. This view is clearly expressed by Peter: "Votes from the diaspora would simply be another way for current politicians to manipulate votes and rig elections. Until the continent stabilizes and rids itself of corruption and other such practices such an exercise would be futile. Besides, stretching the government's budget to incorporate these votes from foreign nationals is a waste of resources because there are other more pressing problems on the continent" (BBC News, 2006).

The ethics of *ubuntu* brought to the forefront by Desmond Tutu (2000) is rendered by *kimuntu* and *bomoto* (in Kikongo and Lingala), both two major languages in the Democratic Republic of the Congo. Ethically speaking, the virtue of *kimuntu* identifies a person's innate endowment with being a virtuous human who embodies such qualities as honesty, generosity, and politeness. Far from being a simple attribute, *kimuntu* carries a whole world vision rooted in a community of parents, peers, neighbors, and close and extended friends. It so represents the essence of goodness in humans that the expression almost always refers to positive attributes. However, since no single word exists to express the badness (or lack) of *kimuntu*, its antinomy is subjected to such expressions as "*Beno me losaka kimuntu na beno*" (in Kikongo: you have lost your *kimuntu* or what makes a human), that is a virtuously generous African person.

It is unfortunate that some members of the African Diaspora have been perceived as lacking *kimuntu*. Opponents of the Diaspora rights to elections have blamed most expatriates for adopting too much of the Western mentality at the expense of African ways of living, which consists essentially of communitarism. *Kimuntu* underscores the basic fact that an African person realizes his or her being by putting the welfare of other members of the community to the forefront, while that person goes on bettering his or her own life. When adopting individualism, the basic tenant of capitalism, most African expatriates might be content with remitting to their countries of origin, which in all truthfulness, some perceive as a favor instead of filial duty to their own. However the size of remittances, opponents retort, they will never supply the welfare of people in home countries who deserve civil and political leaders who know the price of and work for local and national peace, tranquility, education, health care, and infrastructure. With the advent of democracy, only the process of free and transparent elections can bring about this sort of ethical leadership. Opponents of the Diaspora rights hold that the kind of authentic leadership needed in home countries is overall homegrown, and deservingly known by those still living in the countries. For the Diaspora, who have been far from home, and basically out of touch with the socio-political life of their motherlands, to claim to know better candidates to home elections amounts to a lack of *kimuntu* due to personal gain and prestige. The following reactions from the BBC News (2006) interviewees represent the view of those who maintain that by demanding the right to home suffrage rights, the Diaspora lack *kimuntu*. Asked if the Diaspora can vote, Joyce from South Africa responded: "Absolutely not. They have abandoned us to live in the lap of luxury in the West while we must starve at home." Heinz from South Africa reacted: "Why do you [expatriates] want to vote for someone in a country where you do not intend to live—it makes no sense for the diaspora to vote." Lovingson from Zimbabwe declared:

> Most people in the diaspora rely on the foreign media which is largely one sided. Allowing them to vote is letting them vote according to what BBC is saying those days or what they heard from someone who heard a lecture from a foreign professor who has never been to Africa. People at home see exactly what is taking place and they should vote.

Counteracting the aforementioned position, most members of the African Diaspora including Magaisa (2009) portray the very position of the expatriates as that of *kimuntu*, solidarity, toward their own and their countries of origin.

> Naturally, migrants move in search of better pastures in order to help themselves, their immediate families, their parents and siblings whom they leave at home. They occasionally help their relatives and when they get more they extend their hand to the communities. Zimbabwean migrant communities— like the Chinese, Indian, Filipino, Ghanaian migrants—have been doing this

for years. The World Bank reported recently that remittances to developing countries are expected to reach 325 billion dollars by the end of 2010. This is a rise from 307 dollars billion in 2009. And all this, during a period of severe financial constraints around the world. World Bank estimates that with economic recovery taking shape remittances to developing countries will rise even more in the next couple of years. And please note that these are "recorded" remittances. There is more that it remitted outside the formal channels that probably go unrecorded. Our idea, which is by no means new and is shared by many in the field of development, is that with better institutionalization, helping to track the patterns of migration and the flow of these remittances, governments, business and policy makers can tap into this information and formulate policies that help to safeguard and even leverage these inflows for wider development. A significant point is that these inflows from remittances are double or even triple the magnitude of official aid to development countries (Magaisa, 2009).

Back to Aristotle's thinking that one's virtue can become one's vice; it appears that the involvement of the African Diaspora in the socio-economic and political running of their home countries has to happen within acceptable ethical boundaries. The ethical applicability of this principle to the contexts of the present case of the Diaspora elections leads to various interpretations dependent on whether one leans toward or opposes the expatriates' rights to elections in their countries of origin. Aristotle's principle of Golden Mean or moderation requires that the Diaspora abstain from too much involvement and too little interference in the leadership matters of countries they are no longer living in. In fact while the majority of the Diaspora and a handful of their beneficiaries laud their *kimuntu*, opponents maintain that the expatriates no longer bear their African essence and have therefore excluded themselves from a full communion with the rest of the compatriots. The following reaction by Joyce implies that the Westernized Diaspora is ipso facto out of touch with its African roots: "Most people living in diaspora do not understand fully what's on ground in their countries hence giving them a right to vote might not be a good idea. The man on the ground should call all the shots" (BBC News, 2006).

Therefore, the opposition maintains, the Diaspora's demand for participating in the suffrage of their home countries accounts for their eagerness to exert too much influence over their powerless fellows who must bear the brunt of unfair social and political conditions. For the opponents, the interpretation of Aristotelian Golden Mean would consider that the Diaspora provides to their own families abroad while alleviating the socio-economic burden of their communities left in the country, and staying away from interfering in the selecting of national and local leadership.

CONCLUSION

The caveat is that the majority of the expats don't believe they would inter-fere too much in the political affairs of their home countries by demanding their natural rights to designate the leadership of their countries. Rather, they believe they would further carry out their African *kimuntu*, which has caused them to remit to their countries in the first place. Instead of taking away from their *kimuntu*, the Diaspora thinks that their exposure to and adoption of Western tradition of democracy and free elections has added considerably to their African ethics. In fact, *kimuntu* requires that members of the community who find themselves well endowed in any given matter share with the rest of the society, particularly those that are least fortunate. The Diaspora considers their Western education, which might have propelled them to higher posi-tions in societies than other African's, constitutes an asset worth sharing with the rest of their African peoples as dictated by their *kimuntu*. Ethical modera-tion for them would entail striking a balance between their obligations to-wards their families abroad and the duties to socio-economic and political welfare of their motherlands. The aforementioned disparity of views due, in major part, to ethical tensions emerging from whether the African Diaspora demand more than they give back to their countries of origin, leads us to the next chapter.

Chapter Six

Considering Ethical Tensions

Call them ethical conflicts or tensions; they are likely to occur "when we deliberate between what we believe to be our duty and what we might prefer to do" (Enomoto & Kramer, 2007, p. 19).

In cases where two or more obligations are in conflict, the best we can do is to *consider the relative importance of each and give preference to the more important one*. Of course, which obligation is more important is often a decision about which honest, intelligent people may disagree (Ruggiero, 2007: p. 99).

The two authors caution that our choices may be either unequal or undesirable. In the introduction's dilemma of "searching for diamonds in Angola," the nine-month pregnant lady is faced with two major conflicts of obligation toward her survival and that of her children and the obligation to respect the tradition of her ancestors. Her chances to guarantee a decent future for four children she had left back in the Congo and a fifth one in her womb lies on the diamonds that still rest in the inert body of her husband killed by the Angolan soldiers for failing to give up the precious stones. She does have the obligation to a more decent life, which took her and her late husband about nine months ago to Angola in the first place. Yet she also faces the obligation to respect her tradition by not piercing the body of her husband. Additionally, she ought to protect herself and her children against a dreadful curse by avoiding messing with the body of her husband. As those obligations collide, creating ethical tensions, ethicists would caution that the challenge is to choose wisely among those imperatives (Ruggiero, 2007). In "searching for diamonds in Angola," the way out does not seem obvious. Hopefully, the case of whether African Diaspora should vote in their home countries does not present such an unsolvable dilemma. In this chapter, I will describe four sources of ethical conflicts I believe arise from discussions and arguments presented by both sides of the dilemma in consideration. In this specific case of the Diaspora rights to elections, the protagonists may find themselves having to choose between their Western-acquired (individualistic) values that are personally important and *kimuntu* values that are sanctioned by their African cultural heritage. Interestingly, in the present case, those tensions are laid out in the arguments presented by either side of the aisle: the proponents of the Diaspora right to election on one side and the opponents of such prerogatives on the other. I acknowledge that various conflicts of moral nature might be considered by ethical leaders as far as external votes are concerned. However, I have conveniently, and based upon African tradition-al values, made the determination to analyze four conflicts or ethical ten-sions. The first deeming to arise between the African electoral process status quo and the Diaspora's novel proposal, I call "the old versus the new." The second conflict emerges from the traditional African upbringing of the Dias-pora and their current Western-acquired cultural experience or "individual-ism versus *kimuntu*." The third ethical tension originates from whether vot-ing prerogative calls for fairness among citizens of the concerned African countries "equality versus equity." Finally I will use critical analysis to con-sider the fourth ethical conflict between acquired social African ethics and any hidden socio-political agenda, or "ethical habitus versus hidden agenda."

THE OLD VERSUS THE NEW

As it stands, the majority of the African Diaspora who advocate for the right to vote hold deontologist views; those rejecting the voting entitlement are likely to defend consequentialist reasoning of the greater good, as well as virtue-based ethics. For the former, there is a natural entitlement to the selec-tion process of the leaders of their countries of birth for the simple reason that they do belong there as citizens by birth. According to their arguments, human rights and national constitutions (if interpreted and applied with mu-nities) would guarantee that prerogative. Additionally, their *kimuntu* obliga-tions toward their motherlands, which they have applied in various occasions through multifaceted remittances, owe them in return the very rights to choose national leaders. Not so much for the opponents of such an entitle-ment for whom the cost of organizing external elections brings more harm to the greater population that is already hurting. The latter advocate for the status quo (the old) at least as far as allowing external elections is concerned. Underlying these arguments lays the conflict of change from the old way (no Diaspora elections) to the new way (Diaspora elections). Machiavelli has it in *The Prince* that "Nothing is more dangerous or difficult than introducing a new order of things" (Badaracco, 2006, p. 76). In fact, the Diaspora will certainly strengthen its influence over the whole continent of Africa if given the power to shape the politics of their respective countries. The unique approach of ethical leadership Ronald Heifetz (1998) has developed holds that ethical leaders, rather than fearing the novelty, should help followers to confront conflicts and to address social tensions by effecting change. Writing about a bill to grant the right to vote to Ghana's Diaspora, Kwasi (2006) states: "To the opponents, the bill is pregnant with all the anxieties reminiscent of the concerns and fears. They are afraid and are keen on seeing that the right people are elected to govern the country, whose policies would not endanger their interests" (p.1).

For the African leaders currently in power and seeking re-election, a Diaspora's suffrage may present a threat because the Diaspora can use its financial power to uncover the abuses of power that might have marred the incumbent administration. Citizens living abroad are likely to push forward candidates with progressive agendas similar to those in their countries of residence (ACE, 2010a). Supporting new political blood or new social agendas is deemed a direct threat to many African governments and parliaments who fight vehemently to maintain the old system. Fear of the new is exacerbated by the challenges facing many African countries, such as the lack of capacity, resources, and statistics to enable the Diaspora to vote.

For the grassroots experiencing socio-economic and political hardships, adding the Diaspora to the list of voters would draw uncountable negative consequences, such as security disruption, tax increase, and lack of funding for basic sectors of life. In fact, voting in many African countries is a life threatening experience, particularly when candidates new to the established system are involved. Experience has it that a record number of lives have been lost while homes have been burned and voters brutalized in the process of exercising their rights of citizenship (Kwasi, 2006). Therefore, the grassroots is likely to go along with the saying "better deal with the demon you know than face the unknown."

INDIVIDUALISM VERSUS *KIMUNTU*

When analyzing the paradox between individual rights and community standards, Shapiro and Stefkovich (2011) bring to light the dichotomy that emanates from the individual's desires and the search for interdependence. The individual might be perceived as pursuing individualistic desires to be independent, unique, and hold a strong self-identity on the one hand. On the other, he or she is prompted to develop strong human and symbolic relationships. Those relationships create communities, which in turn develop specific sets of social standards for the individual members. Oftentimes, ethical dilemmas arise as a consequence of conflict between community standards and individual rights. Finding the balance between the needs of both the individual and the greater community strikes a particular chord in current African Diasporas.

The African members of the Diaspora reclaiming their rights to elections in their home countries verse in a dual anthropologic and ethical existence that might be seen as fundamentally paradoxical. By their African nature, they are fashioned in *kimuntu* or communitarianism; but by their dwelling in the Global North, they have adopted individualistic behaviors. Ethically speaking, the Diaspora—and some have expressed this uncomfortable feeling—should be torn between full participation in home elections that implies full communitarianism undertaking and their acquired individualism that somehow requires them to mend their private business. The premise of *kimuntu* appears to be so engrained in the African psyche that one would characterize it as being an integral element of the African genome. Elaborating about *kimuntu*, Bujo (2011) maintains that "for Black Africa, it is not the Cartesian *cogito ergo sum* ('I think, therefore I am') but an existential *cognitus sum, ergo sumus* ('I am known, therefore we are') that is decisive (2011, p. 4). This approach compares to communitarianism in that African community ethics concerns itself with laying down norms for ethical conducts as a whole. However, unlike mere communitarianism, *kimuntu* goes so far as to embrace the invisible community of the dead and the unborn. Bujo (2011) also explains that this relationship does not refer exclusively to an ethnic group, but it further includes the premise that the African acts effectively when holding fast to the solidarity with other humans of his or her community and beyond.

In the same token Bujo (2011) acknowledges the challenge for African *kimuntu* to suitably fit individualism. He contends that the African does not lose his or her individuality because of the group. Furthermore, he sees the individual as indispensable since each person has to express one's own ethical convictions. The challenge to explain how one maintains one's individuality and holds on to the community in traditional Africa seems more acute when the African individual has blended both the communitarianism and the individualism societies. Current Diaspora lives in a society that promotes the exercise of each person's goals and desires while emphasizing the value of independence and self-reliance. More importantly, individualistic contexts oppose external interference of communities or institutions upon the interest of the individual. Conversely, a conflict arises when an individualistic member of the Diaspora finds him- or herself in a position to interfere with voting in a community of which that member has no longer full membership. They are called to distance themselves from influencing the political outcomes and consequences of the society in which they no longer live. Yet, the remaining level in them of African *kimuntu* seeks their participation in the welfare of that community, including the selection of national and local political leaders. In other words, if the Diaspora stays away from the election process in their African societies, they remain "second class citizens." Yet, they are morally obligated to share the conditions in the ground of Africa if they participate in home countries' elections. This conflict is well expressed by the following declarations from two members of the Diaspora, one holding the *kimuntu* view and the other maintaining the individualistic standpoint. First Kwasi, advocating adamantly for the right to election, goes as follows:

> I guess it can be said they left Ghana, but the Ghana in them never left. They live every day, thinking, talking and worrying about Ghana. How to move the country's politics and economy forward? They reserve tremendous amount of goodwill towards Ghana. They put their money where their mouth is, by sending money and items such as hospital equipment, machinery, vehicles, computers, textbooks, medicine and clothes etc. back home to Ghana (Kwasi, 2006).

In reaction to Kwasi's online feature article, a reader from the Diaspora posted the comment below implying that expatriates with their present individualistic Western mentality should refrain from interfering in national matters outside their control. "What do you do, if the outcome of an election is determined by Diasporians who themselves do not have to live under the programs and policies of that government?" (Kwasi, 2006).

More explicitly, Hategekimana's refusal to allow mingling with elections in the Global South countries of origin illustrates the deep clash between the culture of residence and that of the country of birth: "[We] African Diasporas are seeking our own success, getting permanent residence papers or citizenship in Western countries. Africans abroad represent a small population of the whole continent and their vote can't have an impact. The continent needs many things and most of them are more important than casting a ballot" (BBC News, 2006). Another reader acknowledges the importance of their African *kimuntu* that causes the Diaspora to remit to their country. However, they sound reluctant to push hard for the right to vote in Ghana, implying that one can only push individualism so far.

> Remittances of Ghanaians abroad now surpass profits from Gold and cocoa exports. They total over $2 billion annually. Remittances are the main source of foreign exchange for the government. Granted that remittances often go to immediate family members and friends, the government/Bank of Ghana keeps the dollars and pays the recipient in cedis. This partly explains the dollar reserves the Bank of Ghana sits on. Living in the US for over 20 years, I only vote in presidential elections. Given the right by my beloved Ghana will be only a symbolic gesture that I will appreciate but have no intention of casting a ballot in Ghanaian elections. We will abide by whatever decision parliament and our brothers and sisters at home make (Kwasi, 2006, np.).

Once again, only the virtue of moderation as described by Aristotle can help strike the balance in the conflict involving the African Diaspora trapped between two paradoxical cultures: communitarianism and individualism.

EQUALITY VERSUS EQUITY

In their *Ethical Leadership and Decision Making in Education*, Shapiro and Stefkovich (2011) devote a chapter on ethical tensions between equality and equity, two concepts if taken incautiously, might become blurry in their definitions. They elaborate on the definition of equality provided by Strike that the concept of equality refers to: 'people who are the same in any given circumstances should receive the same treatment regardless of such catego-ries as race, sex, social class, and ethnicity.' Equality operates under the register of assimilation "because it assumes that individuals, once socialized into society, have the right 'to do anything they want, to choose their own lives and not be hampered by traditional expectations and stereotypes'" (p. 103).

The question remains as to why people of African descent who have deliberately chosen to live in different circumstances than those in their countries of origin should be treated equally with the remaining of citizens? One would argue that Diaspora differs in many respects from people in the motherland: they have hybridized their language, culture, and education, as well as social relations and professional conditions. They thus do not share the same living circumstances and contexts as those left in the country. The Diaspora is so different from the rest of the country that it appears unqual-ified to receive equal rights for unequal conditions. African leaders' legal and ethical obligation to treat all citizens equally can in fact collide with the ethical consideration for equity. Shapiro and Stefkovich (2011) understand equity as an unequal (special treatment), which social policy sometimes ac-cords to groups that have been frequently made to feel inferior to those in the mainstream, and some have been marginalized or treated as "second class citizens" to use Kwasi's expression. As opposed to equality, equity deals with differences, taking into consideration that societies, such as those in modern Africa, have not given equal treatment to many marginalized groups. Aristotle "held that justice consists in treating equals equally and unequal unequally" whereas equity consists in treating differently people who differ on some relevant characteristic (Strike & Soltis, 2009, p. 46). While it might not appear fair to treat the Diaspora as equal to citizens that have continuous-ly and legally lived in their home countries, allowing them the benefit of such fundamental rights as voting might only fall under the register of equity. For example, Kwasi (2006) revealed the painful reality of the Ghanaian Diaspora being treated as a second class citizenry for the particular reason that they are not allowed to participate in the selection process of their leaders. The premise of double standards under which many Africans operate only furthers the clash between equality and equity. For instance, it is common for politicians to court the Diaspora during electoral campaigns to influence their friends and parents in Ghana to vote for particular politicians. Former president of Ghana John Kufour (2001–2009) and late president Professor Atta Mills (2009–2012) thought it was politically strategic to campaign in Canada, Britain, Germany, Netherland, the United States, and many other countries. When taking their campaigns to their compatriots overseas, the politicians don't think of them as second class citizens but rather as equal countrymen with the right and power to swing the results of elections in the country one way or the other. Would it not be fair in the name of the same equality, Kwasi (2006) would have questioned, to extend the rights to vote to those valuable members of the country living abroad? However, oftentimes the Diaspora right finds its place on the back burner in the aftermath of the elections, after politicians have been re-established in their seats. Political leaders, however, welcome diverse remittances "the second class citizens" send to their parents and relatives, claiming that expatriates do it at their own risk. For this African leadership, remittances are free and irrelevant to the development of the countries, and as such have no voting legitimacy (Kwasi, 2006). Although they boast about the many millions of dollars these so-called "second class citizens" bring annually to the country, politicians seem to be lying to the world when treating the Diaspora as equal citizens to guarantee their own interests, and then abandon them when they do not matter any longer. The lingering question of the treatment of the expatriates as either equal citizens or "second class citizens" deserving of some rights like that of choosing the leadership of their motherland is far from being resolved at this point.

ETHICAL HABITUS VERSUS HIDDEN AGENDA

In African political ethics today, one of the paradoxes that exists has to do with current political systems. Our discussion on the topic of the Diaspora's rights to elections has revealed that the political leadership as well as various citizens both in the countries and in the Diaspora has internalized the current political systems through a process that can be referred to as ethical habitus. For them, those systems have stood the tests of time and events and have no need to be challenged. In the same time scholars such as Ayittey (2005), Katongele (2011), and others and proponents of the Diaspora rights to elections have deplored current political systems and found them to be led by hidden agendas. They conceptualize the conflict between politics in the surface and the ideology of maintaining the establishment in power, which discourages many from positive attempts to better the welfare of African polities. The rationale for pushing forward or rejecting the agenda for the Diaspora's right to elections might create an ethical conflict of whether such a move remains "innocently" part of the ethical habitus or it rather supports a hidden political agenda.

Bourdieu uses habitus in reference to the generalized and habitual schemes of thought and action. It points to lifestyle, the values, the dispositions and expectation which every individual of a given society would so well internalize that it becomes part of oneself as a normalized routine. Furthermore, habitus involves social groups' predispositions or pre-determined typical ways of looking or viewing at things and ideas such as taste or values, events, or problem solving. Scholars trace the origin of habitus to Aristotle's concept of *hexis* to mean "habit" that might have excellence or mediocrity dependent on whether it is well or badly arranged in society. Elsewhere in *Nicomachean Ethics*, Aristotle (2007) drew the contrast between *hexis* (habit) and *diathesis* (disposition) for the simple reason that this latter term indicates habits that are more permanent and less easy to change.

In the tradition of Pierre Bourdieu (1977, 1984) who contributed much to the understanding of habitus, I use ethical habitus to refer to the lifestyle experiences the majority of Global South countries, in particular those in sub-Saharan Africa, have acquired through the accumulation of moral values, dispositions, and expectations. I posit that such acquired habits as political instability, corruption, grab of power, and nebulous electoral processes are deemed more convertible vicious values than Bourdieu's "disposition," which would entail permanency. Since ethical habitus points to acquired set of habits in the course of the colonial and post-colonial history of most sub-Saharan Africa, a clear line should be drawn with values of African traditions that did not embrace most of the contemporary social vices and norms. Although it has been deplored in many instances, rampant corruption that characterizes some political leadership has become an integral part of the people's ethical habitus. So have kleptocracy, clientelism, nepotism, electoral threats, and the like. For some expatriates, these ethical anti-values have become so ingrained in the fabric of the systems that it is no longer worth fighting against since one has to lose the fight. Unfortunately, it appears that some members of the Diaspora rightly or wrongly support this position for two unrelated reasons: one they take the ethical habitus as non-changeable; and two they may benefit from the status quo. Voting as an ethical habitus can wear an honest and fair appearance when extended to the Diaspora. However, the spectrum not only of having elections rigged but also that of contributing to empowering an exploitative regime creates a conflict in the minds of some members of the Diaspora. Some proponents of the external votes might be grappling with a question that comes down to this: How can I support those elections that are supposed to be good in nature, when I am certain that the known and unknown (hidden) outcome will not be beneficial to the people? Here is a typical case of such conflict:

> Votes from the diaspora would simply be another way for current politicians to manipulate votes and rig elections. Until the continent stabilizes and rids itself of corruption and other such practices such an exercise would be futile. Besides, stretching the government's budget to incorporate these votes from foreign nationals is a waste of resources because there are other more pressing problems on the continent (BBC News, 2006).

The exterior of a political factor, whether it concerns the appointment of new ministers or the inauguration of a president, contrasts with the ideology of maintaining in power oneself, parents, or friends in continuing positions of power. The claim for the Diaspora's elections rights, whether it is supported or rejected, embodies the same hidden political ideology of power grab, which might be simply presented on the surface under the disguise of the Diaspora's participation in the welfare of motherlands. For example, the seemingly innocent fact of sending their children overseas for a better education might be looked at as a way for politicians to prepare their family for a power takeover.

Kwasi makes the point about children of political leaders studying overseas by sarcastically referring to them as "elite second class citizens." Indeed, they are elite now, according to the current ethical habitus, and might be intended to be elite tomorrow (given the hidden agenda of power grab). "Our . . . politicians who also send their children abroad to enjoy the green pastures often forget that their children can as well be classified as 'Second Class elite'. . . They forget that many leave behind second generation to the Diaspora to carry on the act of living, whilst they, the first or second generation, relocate back home, to retire or pick up some inheritance and or start some business" (Kwasi, 2006).

In the following report by Angus Shaw (2011), the hidden agenda might be even more macabre besides the known eagerness of Robert Mugabe of Zimbabwe to be ex-president only upon death. That the dead have counted among voters in the last presidential elections in Zimbabwe should be seen as a routine political stratagem, an ethical habitus. However, one should wonder if a probable Diaspora's election would not only increase the amount of dead voters and perpetuate a more harmful hidden agenda.

> Nearly one-third of Zimbabwe's registered voters are dead, and others appear to be babies or up to 120 years old, researchers said Friday, calling for the list to be overhauled so that the upcoming election cannot be rigged. The independent Zimbabwe Election Support Network's report said that the anomalies opened the way for "double voting" and other rigging intentions. In its research, the group found some 2,344 voters between the ages of 101 and 110

still on Zimbabwe's voting rolls, a dubious figure in a country where the average life expectancy is a mere forty-four years. The report also cited a lawmaker who found that more than 500 dead voters had all been given the same birth date—January 1, 1901 (Angus Sham, 2011).

There is valid skepticism in the tone Kwasi uses in his statement below, which underscores the conflict between the importance of possible Diaspora elections, national elections being an ethical habitus, and an outcome of those elections that would fulfill a hidden agenda.

> It would be sacrilegious to snub this group [demanding Diaspora's rights to elections] today. Who knows tomorrow they might become the head of the cornerstone and by then we might have lost them forever, as a result of our own unproven and unfounded short sighted fear to rise above partisan politics and put Ghana first. By then the Diaspora would have become disconnected and disinterested in Ghana as a result of our ineptitude. Several things would have to be done to ensure the Diaspora vote is not rigged to favor a particular party (Kwasi, 2006).

People expect threats in the wake of the elections in countries, which is ethical habitus. The hidden agenda for the threat—as mentioned above—revealed a dreadful plan to subdue the population and maintain in power an undemocratic and coercive regime. Like Jean-Paul (BBC News, 2006), most people who find themselves in this conflicted whirl, be they in the Diaspora or at home, might resolve to not vote or engage in political affairs.

> Recently the transitional government in DRC has refused the diaspora the rights to enroll and vote. I sense that they see a Political threat and challenge in the diaspora community and therefore would like to keep them away as much as they can. However, this is wrong; diaspora can effectively contribute to the development of such a country. Preventing me from voting a leader of my choice would equal to an Economic and Political development suicide (Jean-Paul Muana, Congolese in U.K.) (BBC News, 2006).

SUMMARY

In analyzing the ethical implications pertaining to the case of the African Diaspora rights to home country's elections, I turned to paradoxes to bring out potential problems and tensions. Shapiro and Stefkovich (2011) affirm that many of the contemporary strains and stresses occur as a consequence of the tensions that exist in our society. When those tensions are brought to the attention of the readers, they are likely to stimulate conversations, encourage reflection, and set the stage for wise decision making in the future. In the same token, I believe that the ethical tensions discussed in this chapter have been uncovered with the purpose of solving the dilemma posed by the potential rights of the African Diaspora to vote in their home countries. I have laid out four tensions that are likely to occur as ethical leaders, politicians, students, and instructors in international leadership as well as African Diaspora grapple with a wise decision that can appease most of the parties involved in the current dilemma. The first tension is likely to occur when the political status quo is confronted by a potential change (the old versus the new). The second tension relates to the appropriate treatment of the Diaspora either as equal citizens or semi-citizens in quest of recognition (equality versus equity). The third conflict deals with Western individualism the Diaspora has acquired and the remnant of African communitarianism (individualism versus *kimuntu*). Finally, the fourth and more subtle conflict surfaces when social customs acquired over time are confronted by a deeply concealed design usually nurtured by the ideology of the political establishment (ethical habitus versus hidden agenda).

Chapter Seven

Rehearsing Courses of Action

Other people's wisdom prevents the king from being called a fool.

—Nigerian Proverb

One important contribution of the above analysis of ethical tensions stands in its ability to prepare global ethical leaders to the outcomes of the present dilemma. As global leaders attend to both their needs and desires and the duties and responsibilities of their leadership, they are better endowed to predict what might happen considering the intricacies of the question of African Diaspora and their elections rights in home countries. Following the analysis of the ethical tensions and obligations that are colliding in the dilemma, I will move to predict what might happen as a consequence of the complex arguments against and for African Diaspora's entitlement to elections. I will rehearse the courses of actions that might take place and the consequences that are likely to unfold.

Enomoto and Kramer (2007) posit that the process of rehearsal allows the leader to think through courses of action and strategies to utilize in order to make effective change. Both authors elaborate on the deliberative process of dramatic rehearsal proposed by John Dewey. Dewey (1960) holds that individuals use their imagination to proceed through various available and conflicting narratives before attaining a decision. In his own words, Dewey (1960) explains: "Deliberation is actually an imaginative rehearsal of various courses of conduct. We give way, *in our mind*, to some impulse; we try, *in our mind*, some plan. Following its career through various steps, we find ourselves in imagination in the presence of the consequences that would follow: and as we then like and approve, or dislike and disapprove, these consequences, we find the original impulse or plan good or bad" (p. 135).

For Dewey this process is dramatic because it entails playfulness that is essential to imaginative development of children. For example "when children play horse, play store, play house or making calls, they are subordinating the physically present to the ideally signified" (Dewey: 1910, p. 161). At the dramatic rehearsal stage, the global leader reflects on the various courses of action and their intended and unintended outcomes. The leader refrains from leaning toward or appearing to adopt a preferential resolution of the problem. Yet the rehearsal phase allows the leader to move from the imaginative possible responses to actual actions that can potentially be taken. The critical importance of the phase of decision rehearsal lies in that it not only helps to better grasp all the contours of the dilemma, but particularly it cognitively detaches at a certain degree the leader from the issue for a while. Such a detachment is deemed paramount as one looks forward for a relatively unbiased course of action.

Based upon key rehearsal premises proposed by Enomoto and Kramer (2007), this chapter will consider the following questions with regard to the African Diaspora's rights to elections:

1. What are possible decisions African leaders might take and what are the consequences of those courses of action?
2. What are possible intended and unintended consequences of each of the above decisions considered; and how might either side of the proponents and opponents of the election right respond to the decisions that might be made?
3. Have all the possible courses of action as well as their outcomes been fully considered and analyzed? Have they been sorted out in terms of the most applicable and implausible decisions?
4. Finally, when all the possibilities have been explored, what options have become clearer for the African leaders and African Diaspora? How can global leaders imagine the implementation of those preferred courses of action?

Enomoto and Kramer (2007) state that "rehearsal begins by hypothesizing the 'what-ifs' of a situation before acting" (p. 100). We become more conscious of the possibilities, the true nature of the situation, and our own limitations in understanding the action that we might take" (pp. 100–101). What if African Diaspora is not entitled to vote? What if all the African Diasporas are granted the right to vote in their countries of origin? What if African Diaspora benefits from a limited entitlement to elections of some nature? To answer the above questions, I intent to lay out four plausible courses of action global leaders are likely to consider in their resolution of whether African Diaspora are entitled to vote in their home countries. Leaders of African countries and their Diasporas can choose to carry no action; they can decide to deny the vote entitlement to non-qualified members of the

Diaspora; they might grant their Diaspora full rights to national elections; they might limit the Diaspora's rights to presidential elections only.

NO ACTION AS COURSE OF ACTION

A "no action" could become an action to keep the political status quo in over thirty African countries that neither organize effective vote for their citizens residing abroad, nor have the provision for external vote. A few politicians and defenders of old establishments would largely benefit from the status quo, because a voting Diaspora could threaten the cycle of corruption, demagogy, and inertia that has characterized many African politicians for decades. However, the majority of the Diaspora has become very vocal about what many consider their birthright. Some members of the Diaspora see the obstruction to the electoral process as a disenfranchisement of valuable people who continue to invest energy, time, and money in their country of origin. Other thinkers posit that the denial of the right to vote to African Diaspora would relegate valuable individuals to a second class citizenship and deprive countries from more complex debates that can enrich other forms of civic engagements.

Taking no action, therefore, should be equated to a categorical "no" to the Diaspora's call for voting entitlement. Of the African countries that held national elections in 2012, only a handful allowed for the Diaspora elections. These include: Algeria, Chad, Lesotho, and Mauritius. What then does the status quo bring about? First, I do not foresee much activity in such countries as South Africa whose Diaspora massively and happily voted in the last presidential elections of 2009. I caution, however, that it takes a political will to resist various social and political fluctuations in keeping on organizing external votes. South Africa, for example, implemented external voting in the first democratic suffrage of 1994, then bypassed it in 2004 and reinstalled it in 2009. Such countries as Cape Verde, Ghana, Guinea Bissau, and Senegal have pursued their electoral policy as they allowed only personal vote for their Diasporas in the 2012 elections. Personal voting in these cases implies that only a few members of the Diaspora were able to travel home in order to cast their vote in person in 2012. Personal voting stands only for a palliative and a preliminary stage towards a full-fledged voting beyond the countries of birth. This first stage process, however, does well to calm some Diaspora spirits. This is even truer for countries with a short tradition of democratic elections, including Sierra Leone, South Sudan, and Somalia whose Diaspora satisfy themselves with a more or less peaceful electoral process. One only hopes that leaders of those countries extend the suffrage process beyond their boundaries, after the dust of division, war, and political instability has settled.

Second, politicians benefit. In *The Prince* Machiavelli posits that the leader should endeavor to "conquer and maintain the state, and his methods will always be judged honorable and praised by all" (Machiavelli, 2008, p. 62). Although this premise has proved to be undemocratic particularly in the twenty-first century, a few African politicians and defenders of old establishments would largely benefit from the status quo, hoping to get people's acceptance in the long run. In this manner they would keep on reaping the benefit their offices generate without any political challenge. Established regimes fear the undeniable impact of the Diaspora on home country elections that could tweak the outcomes of the elections. Some politicians have even claimed that the influence of expatriates could not only cause problems, it can also lead to political instability. In Zimbabwe, for example, President Robert Mugabe's government decreed that in order to avoid vote turmoil, the expatriates should return home if they wish to vote. In this specific case, many members of the Zimbabwean Diaspora are considered political outcasts who would only land in jail should they choose to return home for elections. This leaves the people in government with enough room for sneaky political maneuvers geared toward holding on to power. Besides, other members of the Diaspora, closer to the highest African authorities either by birth or other affinities, are likely to support the status quo for fear that a direct involvement of the expatriates might tilt the outcomes of elections in an unfavorable direction for the seating administration. It stands not as a surprise that ninety-nine percent of incumbent parties and presidential candidates that stood for elections in 2012 did not act on the Diaspora elections, yet they all won reelections.

Third, the Diaspora feels disenfranchised and aloof. The majority of African Diaspora has become very vocal about what many consider their birthright. Some members of the Diaspora see the obstruction to the electoral process as a disenfranchisement of valuable people who continue to invest energy, time, and money in their country of origin. Matibe reacts to the lack of elections' provision for the Zimbabwean Diaspora in these terms: "The notion that every citizen of Zimbabwe in the Diaspora today has lesser rights that their counterparts in Zimbabwe is contemptuous and demands deafening condemnation" (Matibe, 2009). Other thinkers, such as Kwasi, posit that the denial of the right to vote to African Diaspora would relegate valuable individuals to a second class citizenship, therefore depriving countries from more complex debates that can enrich other forms of civic engagements. African countries would lose the power of creative ideas and insights which only such group of individuals can bring as a result of their exposure to other cultures and political systems. Many Africans living in the Diaspora experience some rupture of ties with their countries of origin and become aloof toward the socio-economic conditions of their mother countries. Such a loss of interest in the economic development of African countries might have tremendous negative repercussions.

According to the World Bank's Development Economics Unit, the estimate of remittance flows from the Diaspora to sub-Saharan Africa was about $11 billion in 2007 (The World Bank Group, 2010). In 2011 African Diasporas remitted to their home countries an estimated USD 41.6 billion at the pre-crisis level, representing an increase of 5.9 percent over 2010. In spite of some significant differences dependent upon regions, the GDP for Africa remained stable at 2.3 percent in 2011. As shown in figure 7.1 below, in the same year the Diaspora remitted the highest share to the GDP of West Africa (3.8 percent), and Central Africa (.05 percent). In 2011, Lesotho received the highest remittances as a share of GDP (28 percent), Gambia (11 percent), Senegal (10 percent), and Togo (9 percent), followed by Cape Verde (8 percent). It is noteworthy that Lesotho, a country that provides for the Diaspora elections, has the largest share of remittances to GDP in the world, just after Tajikistan (African Economic Outlook, 2012).

The remittances funded such areas as household consumption and family businesses. Through their networks, the Diaspora supported various public projects, including schools, health facilities, and professional networks. Regardless of the fact that it has been deprived of its right to vote in many countries, the Diaspora had invested and will certainly continue to invest in the economies of African countries. However, if not encouraged with the entitlement to vote, the Diaspora might lose its current momentum and revert to less meaningful contributions to the socio-economic development of their home countries. Fourth, Diaspora mounts pressure. Claims for election enti-

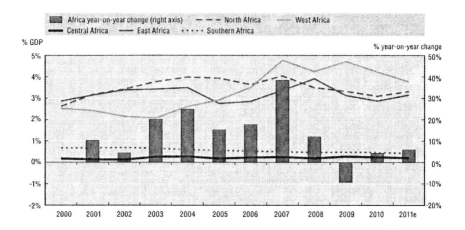

Figure 7.1. Remittance flows per African sub-region. Source: The World Bank (2012) http://dx.doi.org/10.1787/888932600165

tlement will certainly continue to grow louder in such countries as Angola, Burkina Faso, Cameroon, D.R. Congo, Madagascar, Republic of Congo, and Sierra Leone that did not include a provision for external elections as recently as 2012. In fact, the view that the African Diaspora has no right to their homeland elections is also supported by thirty-one percent of respondents to the online survey administered by the BBC (2006). For them, when people leave their motherlands in order to reside in foreign countries, they are to automatically relinquish their right to elections. However, over sixty-five percent of the BBC respondents join the bandwagon of most African expatriates to pressure their home countries for their rights to vote. Speaking on behalf of the Ghanaian Diaspora, Kwasi (2006) expresses their resolve to fight to the end:

> Lest I bore your ears with lengthy narrations that should otherwise be left for the academia, I can say that we . . . can proudly inform our disgruntle politicians that they will have no air to breath [*sic*] until Ghanaians in the Diaspora are respected and given their legitimate right to exercises [*sic*] their human rights. They can rest assured that no matter how long it takes, Ghanaians living outside shall prove beyond doubt to the nation that they are not second class citizens, but we are Ghanaian citizens they can reckon with. This voice of the new generation. . . shall never be satisfied until Ghanaians in the Diaspora will have the right to vote. We will like to make it clear to our fellow Ghanaians that our motherland does not belong to those unscrupulous politicians of today. We shall ensure that they will never have the right to dictate and treat our nationals with impunity. Their days are counted (Kwasi, 2006).

Kwasi's proclamation will continue to be true well after the 2012 presidential and parliamentary elections in Ghana. On December 7, Ghana was set to elect a new president and 275 members of the parliament. However, the Diaspora could not vote. The Ghanaian Electoral Commission (EC) decided that all Ghanaians living abroad who were bent on voting in the December elections ought to return home to register in the ongoing biometric voters registration exercise. Since a new voter registry was to be compiled using a new biometric register for the December 7 polls, the old identity cards were to be cancelled. However, the official position of the EC held that all Ghanaians of voting age would have to return home to register, go back to their countries of residence, and return again to vote in Ghana on December 7. In reality, this unfeasible maneuver comes down to the exclusion of Ghanaian Diaspora from participating in the 2012 suffrage (Ghananation.com, 2012).

RESTRICTED VOTE PROVISION

In their search for a solution to the question posed by the African Diaspora regarding potential entitlement to home country elections, some African leaders may resort to granting such a privilege to a few categories of citizens. As it has happened in some countries, this can come down to dividing the Diaspora's potential electorate according to the length of their stay overseas, their status in host countries, their background, their social and professional status in the country of their Diaspora, and other subjugated criteria.

In its effort to encourage abroad voting, the Electoral Knowledge Network (ACE) (2007) for example identifies four main groups of people who, residing abroad, are entitled to vote. These include: (a) workers, (b) internally displaced persons, (c) professional groups (military personnel, public officials or families of diplomatic staff) and (d) some countries' citizens who have been residing abroad on a temporary or permanent basis. However, the rights to suffrage come with various restrictions for each category, dependent on each country's legislation. Considering those voting restrictions, the various entities of potential external voters can in turn be grouped in two main categories. The first category, which I refer to as situational potential electors, is made up of members of the Diaspora under activity-related restrictions, such military personnel and diplomatic staff. The second group consists of those I identify as temporal potential electors, whose entitlement to elections is restricted by the length of stay outside the country. This category includes citizens and workers on permanent or temporary residence abroad.

When deciding whether to extend the rights to vote to those citizens in residence outside their countries, some African leaders might go as far as to include in the situational category those who are in the armed forces, students, or citizens involved in other official or international occupations. African leaders might follow the lead of South Africa, which in 2004 restricted the right to vote to "members of the diplomatic corps and voters who were already registered in the country and would be abroad only temporarily" (ACE, 2007). Determining what temporary absence involves as well as the parameters of when and who should register and apply for external votes might remain the prerogative of each country. As a consequence, external voting would be restricted to diplomatic staff and other personnel employed by the government. ACE (2007) notes that many countries, including Zimbabwe, already allow this particular category of personnel in official mission to vote from abroad.

The second category might encompass temporal members of the Diaspora who are met by the restriction of their length of stay outside the country of origin. Although this category of potential electors can take different forms dependent on each state, the time limit voters can reside abroad before they lose their right to vote remains a common trend. Some countries such as Guinea have enacted this restriction by allowing up to nineteen years of overseas stay beyond which limit voting is prohibited. Some leaders might include in this category of temporal potential voters those who have stayed some time in another country before they are eligible to vote in home coun-

tries. In Mozambique for example external electors must have resided for at
least one year before the electoral registration process begins in their country
of residence. ACE also states that for the Senegalese Diaspora the length of
abroad stay before qualifying for external vote is six months to the date of
voting registration. Besides, Senegal allows only vote in countries where it
has a diplomatic mission. The table below represents some countries that
have already provisions for vote restrictions:

**Table 7.1.   Some examples of countries and territories which restrict entitle-
ment to an external vote according to the length of stay abroad**

Country	Requirements for Length of Stay Abroad
Australia	A maximum of six years resident abroad (an extension can be requested)
Canada	A maximum of five years resident abroad
Chad	The elector must be enrolled in the consular registry six months before the beginning of the electoral process
Cook Islands	A maximum of four years resident abroad, with the exception of periods abroad for medical reasons or studies
Falkland Islands	Only a temporary stay in the United Kingdom is allowed for external electors
Gibraltar	Only a provisional stay abroad
Guernsey	Only a provisional stay abroad
Guinea	A maximum of nineteen years resident abroad
Isle of Man	Only a provisional stay abroad
Jersey	Only a provisional stay abroad
Mozambique	At least one year abroad before beginning registration as a voter abroad
New Zealand	A maximum of three years resident abroad
Senegal	At least six months of residence in the jurisdiction of a diplomatic representation abroad
United Kingdom	A maximum of fifteen years resident abroad

IDEA (2007, p. 20)

A decision to restrict the suffrage privilege to handful categories of the
Diaspora comes with some ethical consequences dependent on countries and
contexts.

First, with respects to legislations of each country, global ethical leaders
willing to embark in this specific course of action might face ethical lack of
fairness or justice since the basis of the decision appears flawed. It might be
perceived as ethically arbitrary for the leaders of Mozambique to grant the
suffrage rights to members of the Diaspora that have been living abroad for

more than a year. It sounds also ethically unfair that Guinea would exclude from participating in home-country elections members of the Diaspora who have resided overseas for over nineteen years. Other groups of potential voters that face impossible restrictions and exclusions are likely to feel disenfranchised or "second class citizens."

Second, it goes without saying that a decision to restrict the privilege to vote to elected members of the Diaspora has to be met with great disappointment. The ethical unfairness in the selection of who can vote, and the restrictions imposed upon those who consider themselves as valuable citizens of their home countries are among common complaints. As reported by one Ugandan interviewed for this study,

> The leaders of my country refuse to put methods in place for us members of the Diaspora to vote. They have made sure we do not vote. . . . They make it difficult for us even when we try to give our opinions. We have tried to influence the government to allow us to vote but in vain. . . . The government is not interested because the Diaspora group is so powerful that the government fears that. . . we can influence the outcome and we can open the eyes of the rest of the country and we can support the opposition (Student Interviews, 2011).

A third consequence of a decision to restrict voting entitlement to a few members of the Diaspora might conceal some malevolent intention and/or practice to tamper with the result of the elections. Obviously these results are to be seen as tweaked to favor the regime in power. After all, the majority of those allowed to vote from abroad are government officials, government staff, and their families in official mission abroad whose allegiance to the sitting leadership, to whom they owe their high positions and various favors, can only translate into biased ballots. The government in place often makes sure that no votes from the Diaspora go to the opposition. Therefore, restricting the rights to vote to those voters with affinities and loyalties to current regimes only maximizes the incumbents' chances of power grab. It goes without saying that any categories of Diaspora that might lend their votes to the opposition have to be met with insurmountable restrictions and voting impasses. A Ugandan student says it better: "I know some examples during elections where the government sometimes does not even allow people in the Diaspora to send [home] certain amounts of money because they know it is headed for the opposition" (Student Interviews, 2011) One concrete example of a corrupted vote was earlier reported by the BBC in the case of Zimbabwe where the Diaspora's electorate was enhanced with ballots from dead voters.

Fourth, vote restrictions might cause appeasement. So long as the provision for the Diaspora voting exists on paper, voting restrictions might not matter much. Some minds would only satisfy themselves with the fact that certain members of the Diaspora are allowed to cast their vote somehow on behalf of the entire community. That government officials or staff on abroad mission vote would only provide the regime in place with the pretext of having invited the Diaspora to participate in the making of their country's leadership. For example, it might be confusing to learn that officially such countries as Zimbabwe, Ghana, and Guinea hold external voting. In reality, the means of casting the ballots for the Diaspora is either "in person" entailing traveling to the country, or by postal service (understanding malicious mailing delays), or other means designed to appease the international community and their Diasporas. Machiavelli advises this appeasement strategy when he states that although the prince might not bear the virtue of goodness, he should behave and appear as if he embodies it. Given the choice to behave according to virtues or according to vices, the prince should choose whatever way that does not allow him to relinquish power. Translated in our current language, it goes without saying that so long as the people, including the Diaspora, are appeased with nebulous electoral restrictions, the stratagems set up by the regimes in place to hold on to power are succeeding.

The globalization of political, personal, and professional life, the spread of democracy throughout the world, and an increase in migration have all contributed to an increasing interest in voting rights for refugees, diplomats, members of the armed forces serving overseas, and other people who are temporarily or permanently absent from their own country. The ability of these people to exercise their right to vote when an election in their home country takes place has long been an issue in electoral design and management. As the number of countries holding democratic elections has increased, however, external voting has become much more salient. That many more people are travelling and working around the globe only stresses the imporatance of voting from abroad. As elections take place in countries in transition from authoritarian rules, and even more so after violent conflicts, the rights of refugees and people living outside a country to participate in building its future are increasingly paramount. At the same time, questions of principle have emerged: exactly who has the right to be represented, and how?

DIASPORA FULL VOTING RIGHT

A third course of action might be to legislate for the Diaspora's full voting right as an opportunity to voice their opinion about the leadership they want for African countries. Given that people have immigrated to Western countries for lawful and unlawful reasons, the right to election should be extended to those whose countries of origin recognize as citizens by law. These nations would then follow in the footsteps of such countries as Algeria, Angola, Cape Verde, and Mozambique, which allow their citizens abroad to vote in both the presidential and legislative elections (Navarro, Morales & Gratschew, 2007). Sixty percent of respondents to the BBC's survey supported the Diaspora's right to participate in their countries' elections, joining their claim to that of the increasing number of the Diaspora (BBC News, 2006). This course of action might yield several consequences I will summarize in four categories. Diaspora full voting right would contribute to nation building, foster development collaboration between the Diaspora and homelands, promote democracy and heighten electoral frauds.

First, the Diaspora's effective suffrage can bring about nation building. "Electoral system design is one of the most important elements in the institutional framework of a country, influencing as it does the political party system" (ACE, 2010b, n.p). By allowing their citizens abroad to vote, African countries would only acknowledge that their valid citizens are not disenfranchised, nor are they second-class citizens. Yet their inclusion in the election should be seen as a process of nation building. It would motivate those who believe strongly in equal rights of all citizens, and in designing a strong democratic system. Because this is a unique opportunity to fuel Africa's renaissance, policy makers must be careful to understand that all sectors of the Diaspora should be welcomed home. A prosperous and peaceful nation should be built upon a national constitution, which in many countries, includes a provision for external vote (IDEA, 2007). In enacting the constitutional clause pertaining to overseas vote, the leaders of those countries will meet their ethical obligation to rally their human capital wherever it might reside. In effect, the constitution of many African countries stipulates that only the citizens of those countries can vote or contest an election. This creates a problem for those members of the African Diaspora who have become citizens of the United States, Canada, Britain to mention only a few. Although they also hold passports of their home countries in Africa, would it be constitutional or ethical to vote in their countries' elections? This brings back the issue of dual citizenship I debated in chapter 3 of this book. It is left to both the leaders of African countries and their Diaspora to look at the benefits of dual citizenship as an opportunity for networking and nation building.

Second, Diaspora's rights to election can foster development collaboration. As discussed above, African Diaspora has been undeniably a strong engine of economic development in Africa via its financial remittances. However, given full rights to vote in homeland, an emboldened Diaspora is likely to make a more viable contribution not only to the areas of economy but other vital national sectors as well. The interest the Diaspora holds for the development of Africa is likely to deepen because the expatriates will lend more time, resources, and expertise toward development priorities of the continent. However, Akukwe (2009) notes that a hallmark of this support and interest stands for the fact that the impact of the Diaspora's assistance to Africa's development is often small scale. As it stands, that support is inca-

pable of meeting the need of the vast majority of target populations. Therefore, a full right to vote will boost the ethical morale of the expatriates, who
in turn would strengthen technical assistance to Africa. Africans in the Diaspora would create structured, transparent platforms to invest financially in
viable business ventures in Africa; they would utilize existing bilateral opera-
tional frameworks between African countries to jumpstart active networks;
they would establish credible infrastructure joint venture projects with
African partners to help address the immense infrastructure woes in Africa
(Akukwe, 2009).

Although advocating for the Diaspora's right to dual citizenship, Archer's
(2008) statement is equally applicable to the suffrage right: "In the final
analysis, Africans throughout the world in both the public and private sectors
have an opportunity to be 'reunified' which will in turn foster greater social
and economic cooperation and understanding that can be both a social and
economic benefit for all Africans" (Archer, 2008, p. 63). The Diaspora's
rights to election would have positive repercussions on African socio-development. Says Archer, Africans alone have the responsibility to uplift both
their government and their economy, particularly in this new age of globalization when the continent is to increase its competition in the global economy. Davies (2010) argues that many social development actors are tapping
the potential of the Diaspora in order to promote Africa's regeneration. These
range from non-governmental organizations (NGOs) to international organizations, all engaged in meeting such goals as safe transfer of remittances and
achieving the Millennium Development Goals (MDGs). They hope to harness skills for innovation to promoting political stability and reducing inse-
curity. These socio-development actors acknowledge the importance of mo-
bilizing African Diaspora for significant developmental outcomes. Empow-
ered with full right to elect leaders in their homelands, members of the
Diaspora would also feel morally obligated to contribute to various dimensions of development in their homelands.

However, it remains unfounded that the lack of such right would inhibit
the Diaspora's investment in the economic development of Africa. To prove
this, the country that remits the most in sub-Saharan Africa, Nigeria with a
minimum of 10 billion dollars in remittances annually, according to Allafri-
ca.com (2012), does not have a provision for external voting. It appears that
the Nigerian Diaspora like that of other countries has not been deterred by
their exclusion from casting ballots. While a full suffrage right may not
budge expatriates' economic habits due in particular to their ethical *kimuntu*,
it will certainly permit a more engaged Diaspora's participation in the democratic functions of their home countries,

Third, Diaspora's full suffrage would promote democracy. Granting the
right of vote to the African Diaspora is a democratic benchmark to promoting
and strengthening a foundation for furthering African unity. For John Dewey

(1960), election is at the heart of democratic institutions as he often defined democracy in these terms: "a political system, involving such institutions as universal suffrage, recurring elections, and responsibility of those who are in political power to the voters" (Gouinlock, 1994: p. 265). Once more, the extension of full suffrage to the African residing overseas seems an ethical obligation on the part of the African leaders to encourage the democratic process to take place. Given that such a process requires consensus (Habermas, 1991) whereby the voice of the majority prevails upon public debates and deliberations, the Diaspora's opinion would be a positive addition to this national exercise. The Diaspora's exposure to the functioning of democracy in the West via modern technologies and media, as well their eventual participation in the electoral practices, would add a great deal of experience to African democracies that are still in the making. Because of the suffrage exercise, African leaders should expect the Diaspora to become more vocal in their declarations of support for elected politicians in homelands. Whether or not individual members of the Diaspora succeed to put their candidate to the political leadership of homelands, they should be expected to voice their opinion particularly when certain elected leaders in home countries are involved in unethical behaviors by betraying the national causes. The Diaspora's democratic exercise is not dependent upon its economic duty to investing in the development of Africa. Nevertheless, the former is likely to boost up the latter. Because of the economic, religious, and political freedoms that result from a well-articulated democracy, the Diaspora may contribute to bring economic healing and political reconciliation. African governments would be wiser to have engaged the democratic interest and commitment of their citizens disseminated in the world. The Diaspora's increasing attention to the democratic processes and economic investments in Africa would hopefully derive from its full participation in the suffrage of their homelands.

Fourth, heightened electoral fraud suspicion is a consequence to be reckoned with when granting full suffrage rights to the citizens of a country that do not live within its boundaries. Leaders who decide to grant their Diaspora the full rights to presidential, parliamentary, and other local elections would also face the ethical reservation held by other countries that have backed down on that option. Suspicions of maliciousness will arise from within the Diaspora and in particular from the citizens that are currently residing in home countries. For memory, most African leaders have put forward two main reasons for excluding their citizens overseas from voting: the danger of fraud resulting from a loose control over the overseas electoral process, as well as the lack of sufficient national resources to hold external precincts. These two concerns might be taken even more seriously particularly when they are raised by members of the Diaspora whose majority has fought for their rights to vote. Here are some reactions from Diaspora members when asked by the BBC (2006) whether they would consider voting in their home countries:

> I do not know the position in other African countries, but I would say a definite no in Nigeria. First of all, elections in Nigeria are usually massively rigged so that the outcome does not reflect the true expression of the people's will. Secondly, due to a dearth of reliable statistics, nobody knows exactly how many Nigerians are out there in diaspora. If only we are able to organize a fair poll in Nigeria, I believe the verdict of Nigerians living in the country would be a fair reflection of the wishes of the electorate, including those living outside (BBC News, 2006).

The second concern to reckon with, which touches the issue of ethical fairness discussed in chapter 3, is raised by the next respondent to the BBC survey.

> I am a Ugandan living in the UK and I do travel home regularly and send money home. However I don't think Ugandans abroad should be allowed to vote because how would politicians in Uganda campaign in the diaspora?—it would mean they would have to travel across the world which could be very expensive. With the current percentage-based voting system where a few votes could change the result, politicians would use this as an excuse to waste government money to travel abroad to campaign (BBC News, 2006).

PROGRESSIVE SUFFRAGE

A fourth course of action might consist of granting to the African Diaspora the right to election in their home countries under manageable conditions. Since many countries might find it cumbersome to organize many types of elections for their citizens abroad (including legislative and referendum-type elections), they would initially tap into the presidential elections. As opposed to restricting the right to elections to only diplomats or those with official mandate abroad as practiced in Lesotho, Mauritius, South Africa, and Zimbabwe, only presidential elections would be extended to all the Diaspora (Navarro, Morales & Gratschew, 2007). Such countries as Benin, Central Africa Republic, Chad, Cote d'Ivoire, and Tunisia are leading the way for holding solely presidential elections. This alone would provide African countries with the time and services needed to prepare and launch a successful appeal to the Diaspora. On the other hand, the Diaspora would avoid the hassle of being stretched between their obligations in their countries of residence and engaging in many elections processes in home countries. One should anticipate most of the following consequences as African leaders move on to grant progressive suffrage options to their Diasporas.

First, the Diaspora may enjoy a moderate satisfaction. As in the previous potential course of action, the Diaspora would feel "restored to the full citizenship" of their home countries holding both economic and political rights, although the latter will be restricted to the presidential elections to begin with. African countries would benefit from a more active role that the Diaspora can play in lobbying for them internationally, contributing their diverse social-cultural ideas, and participating fully in alleviating the conditions of underdevelopment. More importantly, the agreement the leadership of African nations would reach with their Diaspora would reflect the ethical kind of democratic consensus (Enomoto & Kramer, 2007) or prudent pragmatism (Bluhm & Heineman, 2007) also referred to as situational ethics based upon a historic "casuistry."

Second, controversial solutions will be banished. When the steps to move forward toward full suffrage have been set, most other palliative resolutions that were unlikely to meet the greater number's satisfaction will vanish. For example, states will refrain from granting absentee ballots only to a certain number of registered voters who would vote for the candidates in the constituency where they were registered. Banished also would be a proposition according to which property owners in Africa could be admitted to vote in the constituency where the property is registered. Excluded from consideration would also be the proposal that African members of the Diaspora remitting money to homelands would vote on the basis of their last verifiable address in home countries. Another unpopular proposal is mostly supported by the Zimbabwean government, according to which the Diaspora members who are still paying taxes to their countries, including retirees and property owners should vote. A version of this proposal requesting that the Diaspora pay taxes in their countries of origin in order to qualify as electors would also be discarded as a consequence of a gradual expansion of election rights to the Diaspora.

Third, as a matter of consensus I suspect there will be some measure of enthusiasm on the part of the Diaspora at the prospect of step-by-step vote rights for expatriates, as both government leaders and the Diaspora would consider some practical ways to implement a progressive suffrage policy. Here comes the critical contribution that IDEA and ACE bring in educating not only Africa, but also the whole world on the roles, the methods, and the current global trends of expatriate voting. These two organizations assert that there are various ways in which electors can cast their vote from overseas. They have recorded both countries that offer alternative methods for external voting, and those that limit their options to one voting strategy, dependent on their logistical or financial possibilities. ACE presents four main voting strategies in use. While some are regarded more costly, other voting options are believed to offer a more secure or faster voting channel. Here are the four common options described by IDEA (2007) that African leaders can adapt to their countries' needs.

"Personal voting" comes as a first option. "The voter must go to a specific place and cast his or her vote there in person. This can be a diplomatic mission or a polling place specially set up abroad. This is the procedure most widely used for casting an external vote." As noted above, some countries such as Ghana and Nigeria that are officially recorded by IDEA as holding personal voting either do not allow their Diaspora to take advantage of this method or require them to return home in order to register and return again to vote. Obviously this option would work when made realistically feasible for the Diaspora.

The second option reported by IDEA is postal voting. "The voter fills out the ballot paper at a place he or she chooses and the vote is then transmitted by ordinary post to the home country. Sometimes witnesses are required to confirm the identity of the voter and witness that he or she has filled in the ballot paper freely and without interference." The country of Zimbabwe has a provision for postal voting as reported by the IDEA, but history has it that this option has been used to rig the elections, and allow fictitious electors to fill and mail ballots on behalf of the real Diaspora. Noteworthy is that the postal services in many Global South countries are not the most reliable given eventual unrests and unpredictable delays. Ballots can be purposely delayed by the incumbent regime, and are likely to arrive after the results of the elections have been long publicized. Although challenging to secure, this option would be a good alternative to personal vote whether this happens in the country of residence or any where in the world.

The proxy vote is a third option that could be allowed for people living outside their home countries. "A citizen living or staying abroad may be enabled to vote by choosing a proxy who casts the vote for the voter at a polling place in the home country, or abroad." Many former French colonies have had proxy voting provision for their Diasporas. Benin, Gabon, Mali are only a few examples among others. Like the postal voting, voting by proxy can easily violate the ethical obligation of truthfulness. The ACE (2010) warns that proxy voting can be detrimental to the integrity of voting practice as it allows for registered voters to appoint another individual—usually no-Diaspora member—to vote in their name. The serious downside of this option comes down to a lack of control to ensure that the instructions given by the registered voters are followed by the appointed proxy. The greatest danger of proxy voting comes with the appointment of an individual to serve as a proxy for more than one registered elector. Therefore, it appears that ethical leaders would stay away from the proxy system of election, unless it is otherwise submitted to a tied control. The great rig risk in using proxy voting has prompted ACE to advise alternative practices such absentee voting facilities, early voting services, and mobile voting station facilities for people with disabilities.

The fourth voting option at hand for leaders of Africa is by way of electronic means. "The voter may use the Internet, personal digital assistants (PDAs), telephones or a mobile phone to cast his or her vote. This type of electronic voting is most often referred to as remote electronic voting, or e-voting and may become more common in future." Although attractive, there is no evidence that any country in Africa has ever used this option for either the people residing in the country or for its Diaspora. Nzeshi (2011) in his article "Nigeria: INEC Proposes Electronic Voting in 2015" reports that the Nigerian Independent National Electoral Commission (INEC) was working on implementing PDAs for its 2015 presidential elections. Whether this will materialize remains to be seen. However, the PDAs might be an invaluable tool for voting from overseas if all the parameters that would allow for legal and ethical breaches are properly dealt with and discarded. Looking ahead, PDAs present a great potential for enfranchising worthy citizens who happen to live outside of their countries to participate in national elections. These devices would hopefully stand out as a response to many African countries' challenge to cut the cost of organizing abroad precincts because individual members of the Diaspora could afford their own tools. If operated with well controlled software that keep both the confidentiality of the voter and that of the ballot, PDAS will also come across as an ethical response to the concern about voting frauds.

Unintended consequences would be a fourth outcome of a progressive suffrage. This course of action might also open a can of worms in that the Diaspora would expect to get the remainder of vote phases promised them. For example, if a country provides that its Diaspora would first vote in presidential elections, then three years later in parliamentary suffrage, then two years later in every referendum and national policy, it will suit the Diaspora to demand that the state fulfills those obligations. To avoid unnec-essary demands from citizens overseas, African leaders would see to it that the next steps in the voting processes are realistic. As various as they might be in origin and nature, the Diaspora is made up of a body of people in democracy who would likely make compromise to only one or two kinds of elections in their home countries. The likelihood of reaching a workable consensus with the Diaspora body is so high that demands such as this below can be widely avoided if clear steps on how to move forward with the Diaspora elections are democratically established and agreed upon.

> Most Francophone African countries permit some form of voting ("in person," "proxy," or "mixed," i.e., personal or proxy) by emigrants in either presiden-tial and legislative/sub-national elections or both, as well as in referendums. All Lusophone countries (Angola, Cape Verde, Guinea-Bisau, and Mozam-

bique) and Equatorial Guinea allow "personal" voting for the diaspora in presidential elections (Cape Verde allows voting for both presidential and legislative elections). Of all former British colonies in Africa, only Botswana (presidential), Ghana (limited presidential and legislative; general voting approved
in 2006 is yet to be implemented), Lesotho (legislative by post), Mauritius
(legislative/sub-national by proxy), Namibia (presidential and legislative), and
South Africa (limited presidential and legislative) allow any form of diaspora
voting. Nigeria is one of the few remaining hold-outs (Business Day, 2012).

CONCLUSION

This chapter has presented four major probable courses of action that global
leaders would take to solve the dilemma of whether people of Africa descent
who reside overseas can vote in their home countries. It might ethically be
reprehensible to claim that all potentially imaginable scenarios and decisions
that African leaders and their Diaspora can come up with have been ex-
hausted. To walk in the footsteps of Enomoto and Kramer (2007), my action
in this rehearsal phase has consisted of two main steps. The first was to move
beyond imagining possibilities to proposing actual courses of action. The
second step was to predict the consequences of each proposed solution based
upon Dewey's problems of association. Here I have looked at social order,
change conflicts, and private-public interests as it pertains to the contexts of
the African Diaspora, which I see as the bridge builder between the Global
South and the Global North. The combination of both courses of action on
the one hand and the consequences of those solutions on the other might
come down to the following figure 7.2. Each quadrant in figure 7.2 represents a course of action leaders can consider taking, including the consequences flanked next to the four courses of action. The revolving shape of the
figure represented in a circle means that decision makers would be free to
move their considerations around as they see fit, and that no action prevails
over the others at this point of the analysis.

Although each country would set conditions that suit its socio-political
and economic contexts, they would grant an external vote entitlement according to the length of stay abroad. However, a minimum of six-month stay
abroad would provide enough time for governments and international diplomatic services to ready themselves for the electoral processes. This condition
is set against the backdrop of limiting the maximum time to vote in presidential elections, as in Guinea which has a maximum of nineteen years. Rather
the countries of Chad and Senegal can serve as models of no provision for a
maximum time to participate in external elections.

The latter course of action shows great potential for an ethical 'Golden
Mean' which both the Diaspora and the African leadership win in a two-way
communication. On the one hand the Diaspora would feel "restored to the

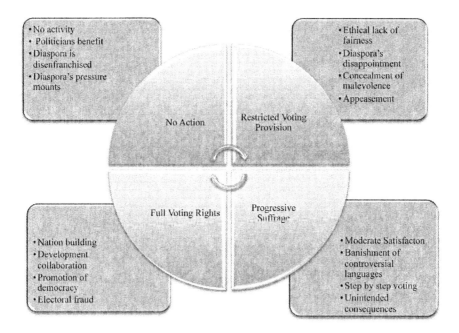

• No activity
• Politicians benefit
• Diaspora is disenfranchised
• Diaspora's pressure mounts

• Ethical lack of fairness
• Diaspora's disappointment
• Concealment of malevolence
• Appeasement

No Action

Restricted Voting Provision

Full Voting Rights

Progressive Suffrage

• Nation building
• Development collaboration
• Promotion of democracy
• Electoral fraud

• Moderate Satisfacton
• Banishment of controversial languages
• Step by step voting
• Unintended consequences

Figure 7.2.

full citizenship" of their home countries holding both economic and political rights, although the latter will be restricted to the presidential elections to begin with. On the other hand African leadership would benefit from a more active role that the Diaspora can play in lobbying for their motherlands internationally, contributing their diverse social-cultural ideas, and participating fully in alleviating the conditions of underdevelopment. With this in mind, I turn to the following chapter, re-discernment, in which I intend to explore any extraneous elements that may account for a resolution of the dilemma.

Chapter Eight

Rediscerning the Diaspora's Rights to Elections

Only a wise person can solve a difficult problem.
—Akan Proverb

Wisdom is like a baobab tree;
no one individual can embrace it.
—Akan & Ewe Proverb

In the previous chapter, I determined all possible choices of action that are available in the current dilemma. I opened four alternative choices: namely, no action or denial of Diaspora's voting, restricted voting provision, full voting right, and progressive suffrage. By determining the four potential courses of action, I increased any chances of making a reasonable ethical judgment. Since the emphasis of the DIRR (Description, Interpretation, Re-hearsal, and Re-discernment) methodology as proposed by Enomoto and Kramer emphasizes the process of decision making over the solution itself, the last element of the process (Re-discernment) is critically important in that it reviews the above three elements to ensure that the dilemma has been almost exhaustively understood and thoroughly analyzed.

At this point, Enomoto and Kramer's methodology diverges from that proposed by Ruggiero (2007) in his book *Thinking Critically about Ethical Issues*. He proposes a four-step of ethical issue analysis. The first three steps are closer to DIR (Description, Interpretation, and Rehearsal) of Enomoto and Kramer in that step one (details of the case) looks closely at the circumstances that set apart the dilemma that is analyzed from otherwise similar cases. The second step (identify the relevant criteria) analyzes the ethical ideals or standards involved as well as the conflicts of obligations. The third step (determine possible courses of action) consists of laying out all imaginable potential solutions and their consequences. In the fourth step (decide which course of action is most ethical), Ruggiero recommends that a decision be made in the light of the findings in steps one through three. Instead, Enomoto and Kramer relegate the making of a decision toward the very end of this step, recommending a thorough analysis of any "unturned stone" by way of a general review of the process. They rightly call this fourth step of theirs "Re-discernment." The task at hand in this chapter will be to make sure that all the important particles that should help to make a wiser decision have been covered.

WHAT IS ETHICAL RE-DISCERNMENT?

Enomoto and Kramer (2007) state that "the process of re-discernment involves discovering energy for the challenge at hand through heightened understanding of the complexity, tension, consequences, and the likely possibilities of any given action" (Enomoto & Kramer, p. 102). To do this, the ethical leader will examine new developments in the comprehension of the dilemma posed by the right of election for African Diaspora; I will only tackle the ethical tensions and ramifications of the dilemma not addressed thus far.

Re-discernment will require that I acknowledge all points of view to better articulate new possibilities and honor the current context. The identified new possibilities might not be completely new, but an alternative reworking of an existing plan or solution. Even in this context, a slight nuance may help to identify why the decision I will choose might be the best. Another requirement of re-discernment is a more coherent description of the problems that generated the problem in the first place. This allows for progress in the dilemma treatment by a redefining and re-describing the issue of the African expatriates and their rights (or lack of) to elections in their home countries. At this point, it is also paramount that I proceed through some sort of individual re-discernment for being a potentially biased member of the African Diaspora. As such I might be leaning toward expressing the view of the majority of the Diaspora consisting of imperatively reinstating this body of valuable citizens in their "innate" rights to elect the leadership of their countries. Re-discernment constitutes a constant reminder of my vulnerability as an ethical leader and analyst of the dilemma in which I might be personally involved. Re-discernment calls for an action that harmonizes the interests and needs of both the African Diaspora and their countries of origin; it assesses the consequences, indicates new directions for both groups involved, and seeks to emerge with an action that might be gracefully embraced by both parties.

Enomoto and Kramer specify that the re-discernment phase does not consist of reaching a consensus or a compromise. Consensus means a group's willingness to let a specific action move forward while compromise refers to finding a middle ground for agreement entailing the acceptance to lose and win something in the process. As opposed to consensus and compromise, posit Enomoto and Kramer, re-discernment bears some elements from both, but it has to happen before the action takes place. Yet its end goal is to reach a greater understanding of the situation as a precursor of a resolution and an upcoming action.

Since re-discernment can promote new habits in the groups involved in the dilemma, it becomes important to clearly communicate the new habits by describing the very causes of the change. In the same token, the original dilemma must be well communicated; so must also be the process of working through the dilemma and the new directions it takes. The real purpose of re-discernment is to avoid the second-guessing that might occur and to help the group work with the new cultural interpretation that comes with an enhanced understanding of the dilemma. To help with the analysis of the re-discernment phase, Enomoto and Kramer (2007) have proposed some questions, which I will adapt and apply to suit the contexts of the dilemma in presence.

1. What new understanding has developed from the dilemma of whether the African Diaspora should vote in their home country elections? To what extent does the new understanding address the interests of all concerned?
2. What new organizational or personal habits are all people involved in this dilemma (including the African leadership, the Diaspora, and the very people of Africa) required to develop to help with in the resolution of the dilemma? In the same token, what are the habits and routines that need modification or elimination in order to proceed toward a satisfactory resolution of the dilemma?
3. How to ensure that the original story of the dilemma was clearly and coherently communicated to the Diaspora and the leadership of Africa?
4. How to ensure that all the needs and interests of all parties involved in this dilemma are accounted for to allow for a certain harmony in the concerned parties?
5. Which metaphors, if any, might help to describe a typical understanding of the election right question?

The above questions, which I address in the below section, lend to the three tenets of re-discernment identified as "reframing" the dilemma, "inclusiveness" of all parties involved, and "reassessment" of the understanding of the dilemma.

DIASPORA ELECTION RIGHT REFRAMED

It behooves to use the metaphor of "extended family" to address African brothers and sisters in the Diaspora. In referring to the Diaspora as "extended family" members, the dynamics of the ethical dilemma in presence is perceived much closer to hearts and a bit differently although representing the same group of people the ethical quagmire is dealing with. The African *kimuntu* (virtue of communal solidarity) that flows through the blood of its children remains active in spite to the divide created by time and space. In his book *Foundations of an African Ethic*, Bujo (2011) explains the fundamental relation that glues so to speak the African community across time and space.

The African "individual becomes a person only through active participation in the life of the community. It is not membership in a community as such that constitutes the identity: only common action makes the human person a human person and keeps him from an "unfettered ego" (p. 87). Many African proverbs underscore this ethical standard. For example, a Bahema proverb goes as follows "Even a hawk returns to the earth in order to die there" (Bujo, p. 87). Metaphorically, the earth symbolizing the continent of Africa comes across as the community bosom. No matter how far its sons and daughters have gone, they somehow crave and return to the motherland because they are all in the interconnectedness of an undying brotherhood and sisterhood network. Therefore the Diaspora, being the extended family remains intimately connected to their sisters and brothers that are currently in the leadership position of Africa, as well as to all the people living on that continent.

This concept of "extended family" includes the members of the African continent that have found themselves in both involuntary and voluntary conditions of Diaspora. In general terms, the "involuntary" members of the extended family of the Diaspora constitute the group of those whose ancestors left Africa against their will about three centuries ago. Estimated at 41.1 million individuals in 2008 by the U.S. Census Bureau, the majority of this extended family has settled in Europe, North America, the Caribbean, Brazil, and other countries in Latin America. The voluntary Diaspora left the continent of Africa after the end of World War II, whom the World Bank numbers at a minimum of 4 million currently living in the Global North. However, the term "voluntary Diaspora" can also be misleading in that other people who migrated in the Global North after WWII could have been forced out of Africa as political refugees, including victims of civil wars, ethnic cleansing, and genocides. Factually speaking, they constitute the cluster of involuntary immigrant members of the African Diaspora. The U.S Census Bureau estimates that about 1.4 million of this population of "voluntary" African Diaspora lives in the United States (Akukwe, 2011). Since they are coming from the same womb of mother Africa, it suits to address them as "extended family," although consideration for the rights to vote in homelands is given, at least for the purpose of this book, only to those of the extended family, whose countries of origin accept as citizens.

The row of arguments for and against external voting is raised not only from within the Diaspora itself, but particularly by social and political powers outside the Diaspora, namely the politicians and the grassroots. Ideologically and practically, the African Diaspora worldwide is torn with the issue of whether they are entrusted with a birthright to vote in their countries of origin. Most of them lean toward the deontological premise that they ought to vote because participation in election is deemed a citizen's right (Manby, 2009). In the same spirit of affinity with their home countries, the Diaspora has taken upon it the right/duty to work for the economic development of their respective countries to which they have poured huge financial remittances annually. The Diaspora's members in favor of voting remained unconcerned about the complex specifics involved in organizing such elections because other underdeveloped countries, such as Chad, have been successful in implementing electoral processes. They argue from a duty-based perspective.

This position clashes with the consequential view of a few members of the Diaspora that voice their discontent against the legitimization of elections outside the country of origin. They base their opposition on the premise that the greater number of people, that is, the African grassroots, will suffer political and socio-economic hardships as a consequence of the funds the public treasury would disburse to accommodate a few voting citizens in the Diaspora. The complexity of specifics involved for the implementation of practically sound and fair elections might be a main reason why half of the African nations don't even have a provision for the Diaspora election.

The aforementioned two classical standards of ethics of deontology and utilitarianism represent what both Shapiro and Stefkovitch (2011) refer to as ethics of justice. The authors are in agreement with Starratt (2004), Bluhm & Heineman (2007), and other leadership ethicists who approach the ethics of justice as an emanation of the two commonly known classical schools of thought. The first school originating in the seventeenth century includes the work of Hobbes and Kant and more recent scholars such as Rawls and Kohlberg. For the deontology school, the individual is central and social relationships represent a type of social contract; human reason becomes a tool that helps the individual to give up some rights in order for the whole group to live free and for social justice. The second school is more rooted in the works of such philosophers as Aristotle, Rousseau, Hegel, Marx, and Dewey. For utilitarianism, society rather than the individual is central; it aims at teaching the individual how to behave in society. Shapiro and Stefkovich posit that in this school "justice emerges from communal understandings" (2011, p. 11).

Among other issues that these two branches of ethics of justice deal with is the relationship between human beings and their state, and in the case being analyzed, the relationship between the individuals of the African Diaspora and their specific African states or countries. In sum the ethics of justice concerns itself with questions relative to laws, rights, or policies relating to particular cases. It seeks ways to enforce or implement laws, rights, and policies. In doing just this, this broader ethical standard appears to be limited in the scope of what it can ethically solve. Taken down to the case of African Diaspora and their rights to home suffrage, the ethics of justice would not suffice to approach the dilemma as a whole. Therefore, Shapiro and Stefkovich (2005) propose a kaleidoscopic analysis of ethical dilemmas in leadership including not only the ethics of justice, but also that of critique, care, and professionalism. The authors believe that dilemmas are best viewed under the kaleidoscopic or multidimensional lenses. Applying such as the ethics of critique to the case in study only complements and enriches the ethics of justice I discussed above.

The ethics of critique reveals that established political institutions in Africa regard the Diaspora more as a threat to their power than an asset for the socio-political development of the country. Rooted in critical theory, the ethics of critique aims at analyzing social classes and social inequalities. Essentially, this ethics is linked to critical pedagogy (Freire, 1970, 1998) providing an explanation for expanding basic human rights, and serving as a struggle against injustices and inequalities. In ethical leadership, the ethics of critique may serve to awaken global leaders to inequalities in society, and in particular in various social classes. At the macro-level, the ethics of critique asks global leaders questions about world inequalities in education, health care, economy, and power. For example, what is the role of Global North–backed institutions such as the World Bank, the International Monetary Fund and the World Trade in enhancing or alleviating the conditions of underdevelopment of the Global South? How does the current economic, political, and military power held by the Global North impact the life of populations in the Global South? At the national level, the question of the right of the Diaspora to election seems very apropos. Other questions might address state or national cronyism, oligarchy, clientelism, and kleptocracy and their ethical ramifications for the majority of people in the grassroots. The bottom line of ethics of critique gears toward explaining social contracts by means of critical concepts including "oppression power, privilege, authority, voice, language, and empowerment" (Shapiro & Stefkovich, p. 16) particularly at the national and global levels.

In that spirit of ethics of critique, ethical leaders would see that the African virtue of *kimuntu* does not remain a mere ideological slogan that politicians can manipulate to fuel clientelism, nepotism, and ultimately power grab by some sort of oligarchical class. Although Bujo (2011) rightly states that in Africa the individual possesses a right of administration of private propriety that always connotes a sense of community in sharing with family fellowship as a whole, I argue that such communitarism has been rigged with legal and ethical breaches. As opposed the "extended family" I metaphorically used to refer to the African Diaspora worldwide, the family fellowship in the African leadership's conception and practice has come to mean exclusively one's immediate family members, clan members, tribes and ethnicities, close friends, and loyal clients. In an ongoing study on the "conception of the common good both in Asia and Africa" whose prelimi-nary findings I presented at the African Study Association Conference (Bon-gila, 2011), I argue that traditional African wisdom does not explicitly foster reciprocity across larger communities as it does the extended family and the ethnicity at best. Furthermore, the obligation for the African leader to enter in a reciprocal relationship with his or her people and share material, psycho-logical, and other social values is not clearly decipherable. One reason for the negligence of African leadership could stem from the traditional leader's divine status that sets him or her apart from the common people. It appears that those leaders' behavior of withholding personal goods and materials from their people has been extended to public assets. The aforementioned behavior of many African leaders, in the exclusion of a few being praise-worthy for their ethical leadership/servanthood, has created social classes set apart by the excessive enrichment of one class over the impoverishment of the general population.

Johan Galtung (1971) in his article "A Structural Theory of Imperialism" explains that an essentially center-periphery relationship exists not only be-tween the Global North and the Global South, but also within the Global North and particularly the Global South itself. At the global level, the center represents the rich countries whose economies employ sophisticated imperia-listic mechanisms meant to benefit at the maximum from the socio-economic productivities of the poor nations or Global South. Rich nations maintain the developing countries in a stage of calculated constant dependency by restrict-ing any means that would render them economically and socially autono-mous. As such, developing countries constitute the periphery that gravitates around the rich countries or the center/core for their survival. In the Global South countries, specifically African countries, the core is made up of the oligarchy and corporate moguls who make up a ruling class of less than one percent of the entire population. The relationship between these two classes is that of exploitation in which the poor (periphery) must gravitate so to speak around the core (rich people) for their survival although the former eats up the majority of the production of the poor in form of services, jobs, and malicious appropriation of the commons, including land grab.

The Diaspora however is another breed of the African shoot whose expo-sure to democratic values of the West has watered down, to some extent, the class differences they might have been exposed to in their home countries. For example, children and clients of African politicians would not have the same feeling of economic powerfulness and legal impunity in the Global North as they would enjoy in home countries. The social, legal, economic, and political structures of the West somehow levels up the various social divides that often characterize people in homelands. Understandably, the Diaspora that claims its rights to vote in their countries of origin is composed of a tiny percentage of the children and backers of the African oligarchy who may—or may not—demand election rights in order to maintain in power current political systems. My guess is that the majority of the eligible Diaspora is a mixture of immigrants who have landed in the Global North for such reasons as education, career opportunities, and political asylums. This whole "extended family" is just eager to see the democratic process, in which meritocracy as opposed to despotism and its corollaries cronyism, clientelism, and nepotism, thrives and favors all regardless of ethnic and economic backgrounds.

RE-DISCERNING INCLUSIVENESS

Having expanded the understanding of the dilemma of whether the African "extended family" also called its Diaspora may vote in home countries, it behooves to walk through the rationale behind the Diaspora's quest and consider the main parties implicated in this situation. In the section above, I suggested that the desire for an equality-based society might be the foundational rationale at the basis of the Diaspora's claim for a participation in homeland elections. This desire must have been exacerbated by their exposure to and possibly their participation in the democratic processes in the Global North where they have settled, which, in spite of its imperfections, appears to work under a meritocracy premise. In a country like the United States it is presently conceivable that Barack Obama, the son of a Black Kenyan father and a White American mother, can become a two-term president just on the grounds of his merits. The Diaspora means to convey such a democratic tradition not only in words but also in practice through an active participation in home elections.

However, among many other objections to the good-society-based reason why the Diaspora pushes forward its agenda for home vote, stands the argument that being such a minority representation, the Diaspora political impact would not be felt anywhere. This argument merely indicates the uselessness of the Diaspora's political contribution in the face of so many other urgencies the continent faces. Says one Diaspora member who participated in the BBC (2006) interview: "For crying out loud, the people of Africa want clean water to drink as well as get a decent housing and shelter. I would therefore implore the African governments to consider this first and forget about foreign nationals abroad voting" (Abubakar Ibrahim, Ghanaian in Belgium).

One only knows that the argument in favor of denying foreign nationals a voting right at home on the grounds of their so called "insignificant number" does not add up. The example of such countries as Cape Verde with a total population of 523,568 as of 2012 (CIA, 2012), of which more than half reside overseas, shows that not all Diasporas are small in numbers. Moreover, elections can be won by a small margin of votes, which could tilt the outcomes in any direction. One participant in the BBC (2006) interview, who vehemently rejects the expatriates' right to elections at any cost, argued that with the current percentage-based voting system in Nigeria, only a few votes suffice to change the result. Discussing the Diaspora's participation in overseas voting, Navarro, Morales, and Gratschew (2007) state that "in most cases where external voting is permitted, external voters account for only a relatively small proportion of overall turnout. Nonetheless, and external voting population may have a considerable impact on election results" (p. 30). The Diaspora number however small matters for the simple ethical reason that, once accepted as citizens by the constitution, the government leaders should fulfill their duty-based obligation to provide the necessary conditions to hold the precincts.

Another rationale for the pressing demand for expatriate election occurs with each looming general elections in some African countries. The topic becomes even more vibrant in the Diaspora as each country's election draws near. More importantly, African immigrants residing in the United States and other Global North countries are familiar with the rights given, such as U.S. citizens living overseas that are able to vote in U.S. elections. Yet, the Diaspora cannot understand the rationale as to why they are denied the same rights in their birth countries. However, one should not lose sight of the fact that the American nationals who vote abroad through their consular offices or by absentee ballots are unlikely to bear a citizenship in another country. As discussed in chapter 3, the issue of overseas voting becomes even more overwhelming, and eventually dicey to tackle, when African leaders are confronted with the problem of doubtful loyalty as a consequence of expatriates bearing multiple citizenships. In a nutshell, one thing is the desire to partake in the political process of one's country; the other is the complexity of the seemingly simple matter of the entitlement to vote while living overseas.

Overseas residents are made up of various categories of people, some with a deeper emotional attachment to their home countries than others. The level of affinities to one's country of origin is relative to many factors such as personal experience with own upbringing, presence of living parents, cultural traditions, filial deference, or even the strength of each person's *kimuntu* toward a *terra nostra*. Ethically speaking, one would posit that the level of obligation due to one's country might be equivalent to one's emotional affinity with a birth country. For example a first-generation immigrant who had spent over twenty-five years of his or her life span in a home country would logically bear more love for that country than one who left the same country at a younger age of five. However, both people in this example fit the classification of "first generation" in their new country of residence. The concept of "first generation" can be subject to confusion as it can mean both foreign-born citizens or residents who have immigrated and been naturalized in a new country of residence or the children born to the above people (*Oxford English Dictionary*). For the purpose of this book, I have chosen to follow the definition proposed by the United States Census Bureau (2010). For this institution, "first generation" refers merely to all foreign-born residents with the exclusion of children of U.S. parents that are born outside the U.S. territory. This first-generation affinity to their native lands remains almost indefectible, in spite of their admiration for the opportunities they might enjoy in their countries of residence. To the question of "tell me a little more about your socio-economic and political loyalty to Somalia, and why?," one student from the University of St. Thomas retorted:

> I am loyal to being a Somali. I'm loyal to helping Somalia to stand on its feet again and to make sure my birth country comes back to the international community, where the Somali people can have peace and stability. . . they can have good government, they can have a good education, good health care; these are things that really matter to me. As far as my "Americaness," I consider I'm as American as apple pie. For me, if Somalia was stable, if Somalia was peace, if Somalia did not need me, I would not be involved. I would be. . . I've settled my life here, I'm happy where I'm at. But unfortunately, when you have part of your body burning, you concentrate on that part. That part now is visible and I want to help out. So there's no political loyalty to the US, but loyalty to the country of my birth is vibrant (UST Student Interview).

Because of the aforementioned reasons, first-generation members of the Diaspora are likely to be most emotionally hurting by the rejection from their countries' ballots. Understandably, they have an umbilical tie with countries where they were born, and maybe grew up, after not only learning but particularly immersing themselves in their traditions and cultures. The African *kimuntu* in them has grown ever stronger over the years of witnessing to the plow of their brothers and sisters and countrymen under the ever unending challenges of poverty due to underdevelopment and unconcerned political leadership. Obviously their *kimuntu* has prompted them to remit to their motherland as often and as much as their economic and professional whereabouts have afforded them. Calling it "Diaspora bonds," Anupam Chander (2001) provides examples of affinity to one's country, which he describes as both the sentimental attachments of the Diaspora to their homelands "as well as the debt instruments offered by a homeland government to raise capital principally from its diaspora" (p. 1013). For him, the indicators of the Diaspora's bonds to their home countries stand as follows. First the Diaspora can serve as the forerunner of multinational corporations that invest in the development of their home countries. Second, the Diaspora can contribute direct remittances to their loved ones left behind, offering charity and direct investments to companies. Third, the Diaspora is expected to show patriotism by welcoming official solicitations from homeland governments in the form of homeward investment.

A slight nuance is to be made when it comes to younger generations born in the Diaspora such as generation 1.5 and second generation. I contend that the emotional attachment of these new generations to their parents' homelands might go decrescendo for the simple reason that they owe either all or the majority of their lived experience and cultural upbringing to their country of immigration. Rumbaut (2001), one of the first scholars to use the term "1.5 generation," has applied it to people who immigrate to a new country in their teens. The label 1.5 generation refers to the behaviors acquired from their native country in addition to assimilation and socialization they get out of their new country. They combine both the old and new culture and tradition whereas their identification stays affected by the experience they get growing up in their country of residence. The level of their loyalty to the country they came from depends on many factors such as the education they received in their native country, their age of immigration, and the community in which they have settled. It is safe to infer that 1.5 generation of African Diaspora might not bear the same degree of *kimuntu* as those who had a lasting and extended experience of their native countries. With an arguably diluted loyalty to their native land, one would only imagine their lower level of enthusiasm in seeking voting rights in home elections. Responding to the question of whether he felt more attachment to his country of origin or the United States where he resides, a generation 1.5 student from Somalia responded that he had become ambivalent as to his loyalty toward either country. He, however, pursued that his children will be full Americans and not likely to have much to do with Somalia.

The second generation would be even less enthusiastic to demand a certain right to vote in their parents' native countries as the degree of their *kimuntu* depends on their parents' stories inasmuch as the latter share their backgrounds with their children. I use second generation to conform to demographers and other social scientists in the United States who utilize the term to refer to the "U.S.-born children of foreign-born parents" (U.S. Census Bureau, 2012). Clearly, this generation has been shaped very differently from their parents' given their lack of experience with their parents' culture. More importantly they have embraced the language, culture, and tradition of their own birth country; their educational, cultural, and ethical values differ

drastically from their parents'. Raised in a very individualistic and capitalis-
tic environment, they would have little to care about the communal tradition
of Africa, unless their parents expose them to those African values through
education and practice. Nevertheless, whether they stand as first generation,
generation 1.5, second generation, or later ones, they ought to be identified as
the African Diaspora or "extended family" since indeed they are all of
African descent who might decide someday to claim some right to elections
in their homeland.

The view that people of African descent sojourning overseas should claim
their shared part of the African elections is put forward on behalf of the
"extended family" as described above, be they first or last generations. For
example, in his controversial article, Kwasi stated that Africa politicians in
general, and particularly those from his native Ghana, view the Diaspora as
second class citizens. Responding to his topical question of whether the
Ghanaians in residence overseas should vote in their Ghana elections, Kwasi
first restated the negative reaction from his country's political leaders. Sarcastically, he summarized his government leaders' position in its refusal to
consider the Diaspora's request: "That Diaspora do not breathe our air, do
not drive on our roads, and do not wear our shoes to know where it pinches
us most and therefore should not be allowed to vote" (Kwasi, 2006). In a
rebuttal against the government argument, Kwasi argues that although the
Diaspora does not pay national and local taxes in Ghana, and generally feels
less the consequences of Ghana elections, it ought to vote. He pursues that
the Diaspora's right to vote is embodied in Ghana constitution if one desires
to give it a correct interpretation. For him and the Diaspora he represents, no
foreigner in the world should ever be more concerned about the welfare of
Ghana than its Diaspora. The presumption that Ghanaian expatriates are
foreigners is erroneous, and only contributes to make them "second class
citizens." In a nutshell, political leaders ought to abide by the obligation to
reinstate those valuable expatriate citizens by granting them the so needed
accommodation to vote in their homeland elections.

In its opposition to the Zimbabwe Diaspora's demand for home elections,
the Government of National Unity (GNU) of President Mugabe goes so far
as to request taxes from its Diaspora in exchange for the right to vote.
Obviously opposed to the motion, the Zimbabwe Diaspora retorts as follows:

"Unless the Diaspora is involved in the constitutional reform process,
which safeguard dual citizenship rights and ushers in a transparent administration anchored in the rule of law, this 'tax for votes' proposal is a fallacy.
The proposed 'tax for citizenship rights' scheme is political sham, unconsti-
tutional and blatantly disingenuous" (Matibe, 2009, p. 4). It is unlikely that
the Zimbabwe Diaspora would buy into paying taxes in exchange to the right
to vote. In any case, the GNU would certainly not be open to the possibility
of a strong Diaspora demanding "taxation with representation" through a

constitutional change that might permit members of Parliament to represent the political interest of the exiled Zimbabweans in the House of Assembly. The position of the Zimbabwe government goes along the line of similar arguments that most African countries put forward to oppose extending to citizens overseas the opportunity to vote from abroad. As previously mentioned, some countries that might have constitutional provisions on external elections don't enact it or only use it for people on official missions overseas. It's noteworthy that most of such officials are unlikely to vote against the interests of the government for which they work and on which behalf they sojourn outside their countries.

CONSIDERING NEW INSIGHTS

Pursuing the re-discernment of the dilemma posed by the right of "African extended family" to vote in their motherlands, I now intend to reassess the problem by analyzing any new information or insight susceptible to lead toward a better informed resolution. The previous section has done well to synoptically bring to the forefront most constituents involved in the debate. The clash of positions has also been clarified. On the one hand the Diaspora represents the position of protagonists of the expatriates' right to home elections. On the other hand most governments' arguments against such a right have presented the majority views held by the opponents of the Diaspora's potential suffrage. Enomoto and Kramer (2007) argue that the ethical analysis phase of re-discernment helps to move the debate in a direction that embraces both consensus and compromise. This stage of ethical leadership analysis can be reached by contemplating information and insight from sources susceptible to help take a more informed and balanced course of action.

Perhaps much is to be learned from the example of eleven countries in the world that allow their citizens abroad to participate in some electoral processes in addition to enabling their Diasporas to elect their own representatives to the national legislature. Those countries are the following: Croatia, France, Italy, and Portugal in Europe; Algeria, Angola, Cape Verde, and Mozambique in Africa; Colombia, Ecuador, and Panama in the Americas. Navarro, Morales, and Gratschew (2007) mentioned that this practice reinforces the connection between the Diaspora voters and the political community in home countries. It enables the promotion of the Diaspora legislative agenda; it allows the intervention of overseas viewpoint in the national debates and processes as far as decision making on topics that engage the interest of the whole country. These authors cited among other reasons for low voting turnouts in the Diaspora "security concerns, voter disinterest, difficult access to registration and voting facilities, and documentation issues" (p. 31). It is noteworthy that those reasons vary from one country to another. In other countries, they might include the geographical location of polling stations overseas, difficulty in accessing the information, and unclear logistical arrangements for voter registration. To my knowledge, those governments don't require their Diaspora to pay taxes in exchange to the right to vote. However, various reasons have prompted countries to extend the right to vote to their citizens living abroad. Although people consider external voting to be a matter of principle based on the universality of the right to vote, the bottom line is that all external voting provisions have been the result of political impetus.

The first historically known external vote is traced back to the Roman emperor Augustus. Members of twenty-eight new colonies cast votes for candidates for city offices in Rome. The ballots were sent to Rome under seal for the election day. This occurred for political reasons (ACE, 2007). According to the same source, Wisconsin took the lead in implementing the earliest external vote in the United States. In 1862, the state extended the right to vote to allow absentee voting by the soldiers fighting in the Union army during the Civil War. Politically, Republicans backed this legislation because they believed that soldiers were likely to cast their vote for the Republican Party (ACE, 2007). In 1975, however, the United States became an exception when it enacted external voting as a response to the demand of the citizens living overseas. The U.S. handling of overseas elections is worth considering. In fact, American citizens who reside abroad on a temporary basis, including the military and others on official missions, are permitted to vote in local, state, and federal elections. U.S. expatriates that reside overseas on a permanent assignment are allowed only to vote in federal elections. In order to vote from overseas, U.S. citizens must complete and file a form called Federal Post Card Application (FPCA) with the Registrar of Voters in the United States county where that national last held a residence before moving overseas. Upon a correct and timely submission of the FPCA, the U.S. national in residence overseas receives an absentee ballot including the list of all the names of candidates. All this process completed, the U.S. citizen in residence overseas can then vote and mail the ballot back to the appropriate county electoral office in the United States by the deadline (cnweeklynews.com, 2007).

On the continent of Africa, specifically in the sub-Saharan region, Namibia and South Africa have led the way in organizing overseas elections. Namibia (1989 & 2009 elections) and South Africa (1994 & 2009 elections) included their citizens abroad in a process of nation building and reconstruction. In the most recent elections of 2009, Namibians living abroad had the opportunity to partake in both the presidential and National Assembly elections. They were invited to cast their ballots at twenty-four Namibian embassies, including those in Angola, Austria, Belgium, Botswana, Brazil, Britain,

China, DR Congo, Cuba, Egypt, Ethiopia, France, Germany, India, Malaysia, Nigeria, Russia, South Africa, Sweden, Tanzania, United States, Zambia, and Zimbabwe. In conformity with the electoral vote of Namibia, the Diaspora ballots were counted and posted back to the country, and the results were announced upon the closing of the polls. However, a political glitch occurred because the results of the Diaspora vote were published before those of the elections in Namibia itself (EISA, 2010).

South Africa has gone two steps further in its handling of the Diaspora elections. In 2009, the Constitutional Court ruling on overseas voting ruled that all South African registered voters who will be outside the country on election day can vote at any South African embassy and/or consulate. Even those unable to vote in stations where they were registered would go to the precincts via special votes at any South African embassy, high commission or consulate outside the country. Reacting to the ruling, the Democratic Alliance Abroad (DA Abroad) issued this statement:

> The historic ruling by the Constitutional Court in March 2009 [to allow South Africans living abroad "temporarily" the right to vote in the country's general elections that year] was a victory for the democratic right of the hundreds of thousands of South African expatriates across the world to continue to play an active role in the future of their home country (TheSouthAfrican.com, 2012).

Furthermore, the DA Abroad, a South African branch of its Diaspora aiming at promoting democratic processes, has launched its campaign to encourage South African Diaspora to prepare to vote in the general elections of 2014. The DA has reminded the government of its legal and ethical obligation to begin making the necessary arrangements in order to facilitate the registration of tens of thousands of eligible South African voters worldwide. The DA urges the government to ensure that the South African Diaspora wanting to register and vote in 2014 are not subjected to unlawful and discriminatory treatments.

Objections to South Africa's move forward with the Diaspora elections might come from other African countries that do not have the same economic and financial securities. No one doubts the economic power that South Africa represents not only in Africa but also in the world. For memory this country is the only African nation member of the Group of Twenty major economies in the world (G-20). Some would find it challenging and even impossible to follow or emulate its progress in this matter. However, despite wobbling with more troubling economies than many other countries in Africa, Namibia (with over fifty percent unemployment) and Senegal (forty-eight percent unemployment) (CIA, 2012) have successfully organized continuous overseas' suffrages. These two countries, among others, have demonstrated how to overcome the economic and financial impasses posed by overseas electoral processes. Brand (2010) includes Namibia and South Africa among re-emerging democracies for which abroad franchise ensures the restoration of political rights necessary for the transition time. She also found that states would include abroad nationals in the voting process in order to stick together a new political community. Furthermore, the process of re-democratization or democratic transition has prompted countries such as Brazil, Honduras, Cape Verde, Namibia, and South Africa to extend external voting to their Diaspora. On the other hand, Brand's research provides an insight on why autocratic regimes such as Morocco, Algeria, and Tunisia decided to offer the same rights to their people living abroad. She argues that political leaders of those countries made it their purpose to pretend joining the democratic bandwagon through overseas franchise; the political leaderships of similar autocratic countries use such franchise to control their Diaspora and continue instilling them with their dictatorial ideology and hegemony. The commonality between democratic countries and their undemocratic counterparts lies in the fact that external franchise occurs as a result of political leadership's will. In conceptualizing and implementing overseas votes for expatriates, global leaders, including the concerned African heads of states and governments, might choose to project light (democratic principles) or shadow (autocratic agenda) (Palmer, 1990).

It appears, therefore, that political will and the Diaspora pressure are key among other factors that might bring about the enactment of external voting. Magaisa and other scholars suggest that this political will is lacking in Zimbabwe and many other countries in Africa (Magaisa, 2009). In Ethiopia for example, "the law expressly forbids Ethiopians who have taken other nationalities from exercising the right to vote, to be elected to any office at any level of government, or to be employed on a regular basis in the armed forces or diplomatic corps" (Magaisa, 2009). The political will was present in Mozambique when the 1990 constitution and its revision in 2004 maintained the provision that Mozambicans living abroad should vote in whatever state they find themselves living. Nanitelamio (2007) reports that the National Electoral Commission (NEC) is commissioned to determine the modalities for Mozambican Diaspora to register for abroad elections. This highly political body is made up of representatives of the government, those of different political parties, and civil society while a twentieth member is appointed by the president. As far as the logistics of the overseas elections, Nanitelamio reveals that the government set aside a separate budget of $400,000, and made sure that electoral registration took place for the 2004 elections. Pressure from the Diaspora and politics will have also been the fundamental reasons behind external vote for Senegalese expatriates, reports Vengroff (2007).

In the period leading up to the 1993 presidential elections in Senegal, under pressure from the international community and domestic opponents, the Senegalese Government convened a conference to reform and democratize the electoral processes. With the involvement of all political parties, the conference produced an important set of political reforms. . . These included a new electoral code. . . and the putting in place for the first time of a system of external voting for both presidential and legislative elections. This new system was approved and strongly supported by all political parties (p. 104).

CONCLUSION

The dilemma presented in these pages has now been enriched with a new understanding, including the metaphorical reference to African Diaspora as "extended family." I have also presented the portrait of the majority of those that are most affected by the dilemma, that is, first generation and to a various extent generation 1.5 and second generation. Brand (2010) provides a well suited summary of the dilemma in question:

Supporters of extending the franchise outside the national territory base their argument on the normative ground that the citizenship of emigrants entitles them to participate in elections. Opponents insist that while residency has generally not been sufficient for the right to political participation, it has long been regarded as a necessary condition. Those who are not directly subject to the implications of their vote should not have the right to participate in determining the composition of representative organs whose decisions are not binding to them (p. 81).

Facing a serious ethical dilemma has been metaphorically referred to as a choice to sit on either horn of a bull. In this specific case, the first horn is represented by the proponents of the right to elections in the home countries of a given Diaspora. The other polar opposite position (the second horn) has been put forward by various governments of different countries with a few nuances depending on local and national contexts and needs, in addition to the hidden ideology of each regime. A sound analysis of leadership ethics of the two opposite positions would only advance the debate by looking into workable models of overseas elections that are already enacted by other African countries. It pays to learn from their ethical leadership in spite of potential impasses due to the uniqueness of each country's social, cultural, economic environments. This re-discernment overview bears the merit of being synoptic while shedding more light on the dilemma, moving it toward a more educated resolution. I have also considered new insights from three specific countries, South Africa, Mozambique, and Senegal, that have had a relatively smooth experience of abroad franchise since it was adopted and implemented in different embassies and diplomatic consulates of those countries. Various reasons contingent upon each country's contexts could explain the initial decision that brought to life their Diaspora's election. However, it appears common to all that the external pressure, mostly from the Diaspora, and political will stand as the basis of the change supported by each country's leadership. Therefore, one would agree with many scholars of ethical leadership, such as Enomoto and Kramer (2007), Bluhm and Heineman (2007) to mention a few, that leaders who embrace democratic principles or prudent pragmatism in their decision making are likely to make change that meets their legal and ethical obligations as well as serves the common good. Re-discerning the dilemma in discussion has provided much more clarity for a decision that can really be satisfactory to most parties involved if leaders adopt prudent pragmatism. The next chapter deals with the final step of this ethical decision making process.

Chapter Nine

Working with Prudent Pragmatism

In his *Nicomachean Ethics*, Aristotle (trans., 2007) states:

> That moral virtue is a mean, then, and in what sense it is so, and that it is a
> mean between two vices, the one involving excess, the other deficiency, and
> that it is such because its character is to aim at what is intermediate in passions
> and in actions, has been sufficiently stated. Hence also it is no easy task to be
> good. For in everything it is no easy task to find the middle (Book II, Section
> 9).

The previous chapter on re-discernment implies that the leadership of
African countries and their Diaspora can learn from the insights of other
nations and cultures. Basically, the task at hand in this chapter consists of
borrowing from diverse minds and cultures that might have expertise and
experience to move forward the quandary of the African expatriates' franchise. The works and elaborations of other ethicists who have reflected on
various ways to analyze and conclude dilemmas can provide much inspiration. Additionally, representatives of the Diaspora as well as the government
leaders that would likely sit at the negotiation table, the African "baobab
tree," could come with some resolution to the question in discussion. Several
African proverbs speak to the power of community decision making or just
the strength of togetherness to generate solutions and actions that one lone
individual would be unable to accomplish. For example, the Bashi people of
Congo-Kinshasa would say: "Two ants are able to carry a locust" and "One
bone cannot put up any resistance to two dogs" (Bujo, p. 88). Different
ethicists, including Ruggiero (2008), Johnson (2011), Weber (2008), Velasquez (2002), and others, have different names for the crucial final phase that
concretely engages a consensus or compromise or something in between,
each with a slight variation from another. Over any other final phases of

ethical decision making, I have chosen to apply prudent pragmatism as elaborated by Bluhm and Heineman (2007). This method seems better suited than the "cultural ethical synergy" (Johnson, 2012) and "democratic decision making" (Enomoto & Kramer, 2007) to conclude a global dilemma similar to that presented in the African Diaspora's entitlement to vote in their home countries. A brief introduction to each of these ethical decision making phases might shed some light to my option for prudent pragmatism.

JOHNSON'S CULTURAL-ETHICAL SYNERGY

Johnson (2005) calls the deciding phase of ethical analysis "cultural-ethical synergy," referring to "creating an end product that is greater than the sum of its parts. In cultural-ethical synergy, diverse decision makers come up with a better than anticipated solution to a moral dilemma by drawing on the perspectives of a variety of cultures. They combine their insights to generate highly ethical, creative solutions" (p. 297). Learning from the example of countries and cultures with a more or less lasting tradition of external voting should lay the ground for a possible adaptation in the African contexts. Citing Nancy Adler, a cross-cultural management expert, Johnson develops four steps of cultural-ethical synergy consisting of the following. The first step is the description of the problem, which entails a clear identification and recognition of the problem by the protagonists. Describing the problem is made even more complex when both sides hold two different cultural perspectives. In the context of the African Diaspora, it should be admitted that the interaction with the countries of residence in which they live has in many regards altered the expatriates' social-cultural and ontological habitus (Bourdieu, 1977; 1984). Johnson calls the second step cultural interpretation, that is used to determine why people of other cultures think and act as they do and to identify similarities and differences between opposing cultures. Concretely, the issue comes down to explaining the reasons why both sides of the African leadership and the Diaspora—understood as two different cultures—hold diverging positions when it comes to the expatriates' rights to franchise. The third step of cultural-ethical synergy called "cultural creativity" consists of elements that each culture involved in the controversy can contribute to people of the other culture. Johnson (2005) believes that at this point problem solvers can generate alternatives and come up with a new solution. "Cultural creativity" implies that both the culture of the African leadership and that of the Diaspora can contribute to each other. It is believed that a solution to the dilemma can come out, which "incorporates the cultural perspectives of all group members but transcends them" (p. 298). Fourth, the step of implementation puts the solution into effect, and gives the two cultures enough leeway for the execution of the decision. As far as the present dilemma is concerned, assumption is that the solution that would be reached and acknowledges the perspectives of both the opponents and the proponents of the expatriates' rights to elections in homelands.

Notwithstanding the merit of cultural-ethical synergy in conflict resolution, Johnson's process appears to work well in individual cases of conflict resolutions that don't necessarily amount to the level of ethical dilemmas, which require a thorough description, interpretation, rehearsal, and re-discernment of the quagmire. In chapter 1, I purposely distinguished an ethical dilemma from any other individual, social, or professional problem, often wrongfully referred to as "dilemma" in everyday parlance. Rather an ethical dilemma involves a situation that compels the leader to make choices that implies breaking some ethical norm or contradicting some ethical obligations (Ingram & Parks, 2002). Depending on the paradoxical ethical obligations involved, some conflicts can present ethical dilemmas whereas all the conflicts whether civilian or armed are not necessarily "both horns of a bull" as defined by most ethicists and scholars of leadership ethics. This is not to minimize the importance of some conflicts of large scale, such as armed conflicts that demand adequate diplomatic or military ways out. The example provided by Johnson (2005) in the following story illustrates a conflict-resolution-like problem that finds a fitting solution through his cultural-ethical-synergy strategy.

> An international relief agency appointed a new program director in a Latin American country who, after assuming his position, discovered that his treasurer had stolen $50,000 from the organization. He reported the theft to his supervisor, the vice president of program development at the organization's U.S. headquarters. The vice president wanted to fire the embezzler immediately and to bring charges against him. The national director advised otherwise. There was no chance of recovering the money, he argued, and the country's labor laws made it extremely difficult to fire the thief. Government authorities were likely to side with the treasurer and pressing charges would make the new director's job harder. . . . In the end, the director went to the thief in private, confronted him with his crime, and then negotiated a settlement. . . . The embezzler was fired for his crime. . . but in a manner suitable to the host country's collectivistic culture. The national director preserved harmony, avoided a protracted legal battle, and was free to concentrate on his new responsibilities (p. 298).

Up to this point, the DIRR method proposed by Enomoto and Kramer (2007) has shown to be effective in conceptualizing the process eventually leading toward a satisfactory ethical decision. The merit of DIRR lies in its ability to help the ethical leader weigh all the options at the leader's disposal instead of rushing to conclusions that might end up being unwise and in some cases disastrous. These authors acknowledge that the resolution of a dilemma may look correct when its resolution is made conceptually from the perspective of the decider. They advise to approach the dilemma with an open mind particularly in considering the leader/decider's "own assumptions and blind spots." Not withstanding its merits, the DIRR relies heavily on the process of reaching a well thought decision without pushing farther to the concreteness of the course of action, which ultimately represents the outcome of this intellectual exercise. The passage from the last phase of DIRR, Re-discernment, to the resolution of the dilemma resembles a computer engineering of a machine without a concrete shop assemblage of all the parts. Many students in international and educational leadership programs that were required to test this approach in professional case studies stumbled with the "factoring" of the course of action. The way to finalize this process and funneling it into a workable course action needs to look into prudent pragmatism.

PRUDENT PRAGMATISM

Prudent pragmatism presents a more contextualized and hands-on path to some sort of applicable course of action with regard to the question of the African Diaspora franchise. I see it as an end-game strategy following the foundational and critical analysis of the case. Ethical foundations remain invaluable given that they are destined to deconstruct the dilemma to ensure that it has been thoroughly and properly looked upon to the limit of human and ethical abilities. I do not see prudent pragmatism as a substitution to the DIRR process that has led the discussion to this point. Rather it complements the DIRR in a harmonious way while bringing the dilemma to a malleable closing point, constituting a more down-to-earth ethical reconstructing phase. In their recent article titled "What Is Prudent Pragmatism?," Bluhm and Heineman (2007) propose this novel standard of ethical analysis as a consequence of the disillusion ethicists and philosophers including the authors themselves have experienced in the classic standards of ethical analysis, namely consequentialism/utilitarianism (J. Stuart Mill: 1806–1873; J. Bentham: 1748–1832) and deontology (represented by I. Kant: 1724–1804). In the abstract to the aforementioned article, an editor's comment reads "William Bluhm & Robert Heineman (2007) show how to do ethics without foundations," which is certainly not the ambition of the current analysis that has laid out all the classical ethical standards applicable to the case of the Diaspora rights to homeland suffrage. These authors explain:

> Prudent pragmatism is a situational ethic. It draws the principles relevant to a decision from the facts of the particular case. Historically, this method has been known by the name of "casuistry." Early versions of it are found in the jurisprudence of the lawyers who constructed the Roman *Jus Gentium* [the Laws of the Peoples] and in the body of principles built up by the rabbinical schools out of the moral experience of ancient Israel (p. 31).

Case method or prudent pragmatism, as Bluhm and Heineman (2007) in *Ethics and Public Policy: Methods and Cases* refer to their ethical standard, originated as a means of policy and ethics analysis from Aristotle and ancient Greek philosophers. For memory, Aristotle distinguishes between pure reason and practical reason. With pure reason, people understand the world of the universals within the material world. Practical reason requires that a person develops virtues particularly that of moderation, which in other words stands for acting in accordance to the mean. Additionally, practical reason calls for the virtue of prudence, which in turn demands much hands-on experience. It urges humans to be doers "who have a feel for facts, for varying circumstances" (p. 28). According to this understanding, Aristotle posits that the good physician is the one who knows from his or her experience, as opposed to knowing exclusively from the abstract, that white meat is good for the patient and prescribe it.

Down to the Diaspora rights to election, after abstractedly deconstructing the dilemma by means of DIRR, it is only fitting that the ethical leader now moves to a concrete prescription of a resolution. This requires calling upon moderation, prudence, experts' experience as well as a mastery of which facts are relevant and what rules should be applied to particular circumstances. Bluhm and Heineman cite the example provided by ethicist Julius Kovesi in his 1967 book *Moral Nations*, distinguishing universal moral ideas from their practical interpretation. It is one thing to know broadly that government leaders are legally and ethically obligated to the implementation of franchise for their citizens, but prudent pragmatism (borrowing from Kovesi's form of casuistry) provides a means of deciding how to apply such "universal." Kovesi argues that in some cases for example lying would mean intentional fooling of people, in other cases it would come down to "a saving deceit" when lying can save the life of a person. In the same token, killing as a universal construct can mean both vicious murder and legal execution. Applied to the Diaspora franchise, ensuring elections without fraud or financial burden (to the country economy) remains an ideal for African heads of states. Yet providing Diaspora franchise can generate increased scrutiny (from the independent observers) and massive flow of remittances (from expatriates). A prudent pragmatist leader would find that the universal, that is clean election, when brought down to a particular case, namely external rights to vote for African "extended family," is not only deemed conceivable, but it is rather doable. The prudent pragmatist ethical leader is someone who can distinguish and solve these few sample cases, to which neither utilitarianism nor deontology can provide a proper resolution.

At the heart of prudent pragmatism features deliberative/discursive democracy, a move toward a participatory pole of the spectrum, engaging more public interests so needed for active citizenship (p. 50). Citing John Dryzek, a proponent of deliberative democracy, Bluhm and Heineman (2007) tell us that deliberative democracy embraces Aristotelian practical reason, involving "persuasion, reflection upon values, prudent judgment, and free disclosure of one's ideas" (p. 50). For him, these authors pursue, discursive democracy embodies "communicative rationality." The latter feature of prudent pragmatism takes the shape of a discourse between concerned people, which can lead to principles of action and potential means to achieve concrete acts. As Bluhm and Heineman (2007) state: "If we wish to be prudent pragmatists in our public decision making, we must learn to practice deliberative democracy. . . we must consult our virtues as citizens, not as consumers, because our canvass of an issue is not to the end of satisfying a preference, but of deciding what kind of policy is for the common good" (p. 61). Thus, the rupture within the Diaspora on the one hand and the tensions between political leaders and the Diaspora on the other hand with regard to whether or not the African Diaspora should hold the right to vote in their native countries, might be solved in the lens of the ethical process identified as prudent pragmatism. Application of prudent pragmatism will require that both African governments and their respective Diasporas set aside their personal interests to work toward the social-political development of their country.

The original coinage of deliberative democracy is attributed to Joseph M. Bessette (1980) who used it in his book chapter "Deliberative Democracy: The Majority Principle in Republican Government" to express the insufficiency of the mere exercise of voting as a means of reaching legitimacy in a democratic decision making. Proponents of this process argue that deliberative democracy is a better instrument for decision making. Furthermore, decisions that are made through this process are more effective, better judged, and morally sound. Deliberative democracy gives the opportunity to review the reason behind a particular view. It does not base the final decision solely on the preferences of those who had a chance to vote. Reasons must be publicly discussed, and not one reason should be arbitrary rejected. As such discursive democracy encompasses elements from both consensus decision making and majority rule. It is different from traditional democracy in that mere voting is not the primary source of legitimacy for the law, but rather deliberation. Among ideal models of democratic deliberation, scholars often cite the jury system in criminal trials.

Although not explicitly explored by Bluhm and Heineman (2007), prudent pragmatism finds a strong connection to Habermas' elaboration of discursive democracy and public sphere. For him the political system is not a means of compiling or sorting individual preferences out. Rather, it is an open space aiming at changing opinions by means of public debate and civil confrontation. It is a sort of participatory democracy whose central element features deliberation. Therefore, prudent pragmatism is an instrument of persuasion rather than coercion, and an instrument whereby deliberation with others gets enriched. Habermas understands public sphere as a space where the different strata of a citizenry exchange ideas and discuss issues, in order to reach agreement about "matters of general interest" (Habermas, 1991). Fraser (1990) rephrases Habermas' conception of the public sphere, making it more applicable to our current contexts. She writes: [By public sphere, Habermas]

> designates a theater in modern societies in which political participation is enacted through the medium of talk. It is a space in which citizens deliberate about their common affairs, hence, an institutionalized arena of discursive interaction. This arena is conceptually distinct from the state; it is a site for the production and circulation of discourses that can in principle be critical of the state. The public sphere in Habermas's sense is also conceptually distinct from the official-economy; it is not an arena of market relations but rather one of discursive relations, a theater of debating and deliberating rather than for buying and selling. Thus, this concept of the public sphere permits us to keep in view distinctions between state apparatuses, economic markets, and democratic associations, distinctions that are essential to democratic theory (p. 57).

To solve the question of whether the people from African descent residing outside their countries can participate in the suffrage of their home countries, global leaders can find the process of prudent pragmatism very useful. However, the aforementioned elements of this concept, including deliberative democracy and public sphere, are not so foreign to the richness of African cultures and traditions. Ayittey (1998) underscores the existence of some African "public sphere" calling it the African "village meeting under a big tree," which he compares to the European Parliament. He argues that the African had participatory democracy whereas the European introduced parliamentary democracy. Openness and inclusiveness constituted the main features of what Ayittey refers to as "Africa's indigenous system of government" (p. 91). The decision-making process involved everyone because participation did not require affiliation to a political party or ethnic provenance. More importantly, "At village meetings, the people expressed their views freely, which was vital for consensus to be reached. No one was arrested or detained for disagreeing with the chief" (p. 92).

AFRICAN "BAOBAB TREE"

Like in traditional Africa when a village would unite under a "baobab tree" to settle critical issues of a socio-political nature, both the Diaspora and African leadership would reflect on the importance and the means to extend external voting to valuable citizens who have kept affinity ties with their motherland (Ayittey, 2005). The starting point of any productive discussion ought to be a friendly meeting where the African leadership would sit with the Diaspora to discuss this matter of national importance. For this to happen, the conveners to the meeting are required to bear qualities of ethical/servant leadership (Northouse, 2010) particularly that of respect of others by listening intently to their opinions. Like in the old African "baobab tree," both the national and Diaspora leaders have to bear in mind that the ultimate purpose of the "extended family" gathering comes down to serving others, including all their citizens within and outside the boundaries of their countries. They would come to the "village meeting" armed with justice for all, knowing that the question of fairness and equity will be at the core of the discussions. Discussions should be based on honesty and authenticity, without hidden agenda to promote certain ideology or the hegemony of the ruling party. The community that will be built under the "baobab tree" is to become a microcosm of the whole country: conveners come together with the determination to build or re-empower their country, making it a more livable and inclusive place. The above prerequisites are only the premise of an irreplaceable two-way communication between the national leadership of concerned countries with their specific Diasporas. This public sphere would allow the conveners to raise and analyze the disadvantages and advantages of holding elections outside the country for their expatriates.

First, the review of the disadvantages would consist of laying out the variety of the main objections to the Diaspora's right to elections, which I might sum up into five categories.

1) Failure for people living abroad to pay taxes to the motherland has constituted an objection specifically raised by the government of Zimbabwe, and some citizens living in the country.
2) Ignorance of candidates to the political positions and ignorance of their social views has been another reason to deny the Diaspora franchise. Objectors' argument charges that without knowledge of the candidates to official offices or the issues they stand for, the Diaspora should be deemed incapacitated to vote.
3) Others have argued that the challenge to track and assess the Diaspora throughout the world, especially when people change professions, addresses, and countries, constitutes a sufficient reason to drop the Diaspora's franchise altogether.
4) A major impasse to the implementation of the Diaspora's franchise has consisted of the cost of preparing extra ballots and shipping and handling them to different countries where the Diaspora might reside.
5) Risk of delay and therefore of fraud when mailing and counting real ballots stands as another major impasse to the external suffrage.

Kwasi (2006) metaphorically encapsulates a Ghanaian population's objection to its Diaspora's election in these terms: "That Diaspora do not breathe our air, do not drive on our roads, and do not wear our shoes to know where it pinches us most and therefore should not be allowed to vote" (Kwasi, 2006, p. 2).

Against this backdrop, conveners would consider many advantages of external elections as offered by countries such as Botswana, France, Mali, Senegal, and the United States that have held them in the recent past. They evoke the following advantages.

1) Welcoming the "extended family" and recognizing the Diaspora's freedom of expression and birthright of citizenship has been considered most rewarding for the citizens both in the country and overseas.
2) Participation in democratic processes through franchise and deliberative democracy is of national interest. As a brain gain or brain circulation power, the Diaspora can really contribute to a multifaceted empowerment of the country.
3) The suffrage process would enhance in the Diaspora a feeling of duty, a habit of co-operation and interdependence.
4) The Diaspora would enrich the social political debates with their overseas experience of lived democracy.
5) This extended family will be encouraged to bring additional international ideas, investment, and capital.
6) It might provide checks and balances, and would ensure the rule of law and accountability for all.

The previous chapter analyzed four possible courses of option which leaders might consider as they grapple with the dilemma of external franchise. After re-discerning those options in chapter 8, and reconstructing them by means of prudent pragmatism, it dawns on me that the best balanced option comes down to granting progressive suffrage to the African Diaspora. The use of "African baobab tree" process or prudent pragmatism would certainly allow both the African leadership and its Diaspora to consider seriously extending the voting right to their fellow men and women living overseas. Granting the Diaspora a progressive franchise as described in chapter 7 (see option 4) stands up as the wiser option, most likely to win the conveners' consensus and compromise. I would, therefore, suggest to start with the presidential elections for a certain number of years before moving to parliamentary, referendum-type, and other local elections or considering the parliamentary representation of those citizens living abroad. As described by the legal system of each country, the franchise right would primarily be extended only to citizens whose countries of origin recognize as such, although countries have granted this right indiscriminately to all their citizens abroad for various reasons.

Brand (2010) contends that extending franchise abroad is not a novelty, and a country government does not have to be democratic to grant its expatriates the right to vote overseas. She suggests that many autocratic countries have used the voting system abroad to control their Diaspora and impose their hegemony. I might also posit that leaders of African countries that are so adamant in their refusal to allow their expatriates overseas voting rights might do it for the same outcomes as those political leaders who have granted that right to their Diaspora. In spite of the divergence in the means democratic and undemocratic leaders might utilize to reach out (or not) to their expatriates, the end goal might remain that of maintaining themselves in power at any cost. On the one hand, a voting Diaspora might help to attain that outcome; on the other hand, a non-voting Diaspora can also be used as a mechanism for some leaders to hold on to power. In any case, Machiavelli's (2005) lesson well serves leaders with unethical intentions to help themselves and keep the power by any means:

> One must understand this: a prince, and especially a new prince, cannot observe all those things for which men are considered good, because in order to maintain the state he must often act against his faith, against charity, against humanity, and against religion. And so it is necessary that he should have a mind ready to turn itself according to the way the winds of Fortune and the changing circumstances command him. And, as I said above, he should not depart from the good if it is possible to do so, but he should know how to enter into evil when forced by necessity (p. 61).

Likely the process utilized in this book is based upon ethical leadership premises, and the ultimate prerequisite to a successful prudent pragmatism that I have explained above presupposes the integrity of intent and honesty as required by the core principles of ethical leadership (Northouse, 2010).

Leading with Respect

In granting a progressive suffrage to the Diaspora, ethical leaders of Africa would show respect not only to the expatriates, but also to their entire people. Ethicists that hold deontological views, including philosopher Immanuel Kant (1724–1804) argue that it is a human obligation to treat others with humanity and respect. Respect here means that the African leaders treat all their citizens including those who live overseas as ends in themselves and not as means to ends. This happens when the leadership is able to listen closely to their followers, is emphatic, and tolerant of opposing points of view. Respecting their people means for the leadership "treating subordinates in ways that confirm their beliefs, attitudes, and values" (Northouse, 2010, p. 388). It is in the essence of humanity that the African leaders hold their own individual visions and goals that might not match those set forth for the entire people. In the case of overseas franchise, opportunity is offered for such leaders to exert ethical leadership and treat the Diaspora's decisions and values with respect, in other words treating them as ends not as means to the leader's ends. When ethical leaders, like those that would agree to gather beneath "the baobab tree," exhibit respect to the expatriates, the Diaspora can feel competent about their support to the homeland. In showing respect, African leaders would treat the Diaspora as both worthy human beings and citizens.

Leading with Stewardship

In extending a progressive suffrage to their Diaspora, African leaders will practice the virtue of service or stewardship. Many scholars of leadership ethics, including Gilligan (1982) and Greenleaf (1977) have maintained that the primary engine of ethical leadership is service to others. For Senge (1990) the stewardship of a leader consists of clarifying and nurturing the vision set forth for the people, a vision that is greater than individual ambitions of the leader. Greenleaf (1977) added the important aspect of waiting on the have-nots to the heart of servant leadership. This principle of a leader as servant and custodian of the commons needs particular attention as far as the African leadership is concerned. In a paper on "Understanding the Disparity between African and Asian Conception of the Common Good: Leadership Implication for Social-Development" I presented at the African Studies Association, I maintained the following. One of the tenets of African morality pertaining to the common good is "the greatest happiness and good of the tribe" as the "end and aim of each member of the tribe," including the governing rulers (Gyekye, 2010). The standard of well-being, which includes economic happiness, is therefore utilitarian in African tradition. However, the governing body does not seem to hold the duty of ensuring economic sustenance of the people. Rather, food is provided to all by "He who supplies the needs of His creatures," understanding the higher being or God (Mbiti, 1992). By virtue of their office, African kings, queens, and rulers where they exist, "are not simply political heads: they are the mystical and religious heads, the divine symbol of their people's health and welfare" (Mbiti, p. 177). As such, African traditional rulers expect not only veneration and respect, but also tribute and booties in terms of foods and other material favors. One would also note the duty of assisting economically the members of one's tribe/ethnicity understood as the largest human community beyond the immediate extended family. Tarimo (2008) explains that in Africa ethnic identity refers to a group of people with common ancestry, language, symbol, and territory. The foundation of ethnic identity can be found in combined memories of the past and common expectations. Therefore, the African conception of service and stewardship as applied to economic duties bifurcates from that of Confucianism. On the one hand Confucian teaching compels Asian rulers to care for the economic welfare of their polity, which encompasses not just the ethnicity but also the state. On the other hand, traditional African rulers only bear the human brotherhood to provide for their community, which does not imply the larger polity, such as the country.

It is critically important for the whole leadership assembled at the "baobab tree" to be cognizant about the less than favorable conception of service and stewardship in the traditional Africa, in order for them to serve rather than being served. Yet African leaders under the "baobab tree" will see to it that the vision of moving their country in a social economic welfare requires tapping the expertise and energy of the Diaspora. Extending the suffrage to the expatriates becomes a practical expression that their hopes and expectations for their homeland have been attentively listened to. So are the needs of the people back home who expect more support from their "extended family" residing overseas. The implementation of the principle of service makes the African leaders become follower centered, for placing the interests of their citizenry, including the Diaspora, foremost in their work.

Leading with Justice and Fairness

The extension of the progressive suffrage to the Diaspora will be a testimonial to the justice and fairness of African leaders' political will. An ethical leader practicing justice also places fairness at the center of the leader's decision making. The notions of justice and fairness work alongside each other, implying that no one should receive special treatment in normal conditions, except when an individual's particular situations demand it. The justice and fairness principles should vindicate the African leaders who extend the right to vote to their Diaspora. Although these might not pay taxes to the country or live the outcomes of elections, it sounds fair to value their multifaceted support of their homeland and treat them as equal citizens. The core deontological and moral standard, held by most ethicists such as Kant, Rawls (1971), Shapiro and Stefkovich (2011), and others, calls for reciprocity that is translated in the Golden Rule: "Do unto others as you would have them do unto you." In extending the right to vote to their Diaspora, ethical leaders of Africa put themselves in the expatriates' shoes, since they too would have been fulfilled to participate in their homelands' franchise. In fact most African leaders had themselves been in the Diaspora before holding the highest offices in their homelands. One would think about Léopold Sédar Senghor (Senegal), Kwame Nkrumah (Ghana), John Dramani Mahama (Ghana), Julius Nyerere (Tanzania), Ellen Johnson Sirleaf (Liberia), to mention only a few. The principles of distributive justice outlined by Beauchamp and Bowie (1988) (table 9.1) can serve as guidelines to the ethical leaders in assessing fairly the benefits and burdens of external franchise.

Table 9.1. Principles of Distributive Justice

These principles are applied in different situations.
- To each person
- An equal share or opportunity
- According to individual need
- According to that person's rights
- According to individual effort
- According to societal contribution
- According to merit or performance

Northouse (2010), p. 390.

Leading with Honesty

Leading with honesty is another core feature of ethical leadership, which the conveners under the "baobab tree" ought to embody when deciding to extend franchise to the Diaspora. In his book, *The Ethical Imperative*, Dalla Costa (1998) argues about what it means for leaders in organizations to be honest. He states that being honest for the leader means the following: promising only what he or she can deliver; representing facts accurately; being upright by avoiding to hide "behind spin-doctored evasions"; embracing obligations; opening up to accountability; and ensuring that business pressures from the most powerful do not excuse the leader from the responsibility to respect the dignity and humanity of one another. Foremost, an ethical leader "recognizes and acknowledges "the necessity of honesty and rewards honest behavior within the organization" (Northouse, p. 392). An agreement to extend the right to suffrage becomes an ethical obligation to deliver. Hopefully, African leaders under the "baobab tree" would not only agree on the rights to home elections for their expatriates as a sign of professional honesty, they will also deliver on their promise by putting in place the necessary infrastructures for the external suffrage to take shape. They might set up an accountability system or committee to make sure that the agreement clauses with regard to the expatriates' elections are met in the very next homeland suffrage. Working with honesty implies for the ethical leaders to be authentic and sensitive to the attitudes and feelings of followers. As opposed to the case presented by Brand (2010) in which some autocratic regimes in the Global South offer election rights to their Diaspora in order to exert control over them, the ethical leaders under the "baobab tree" would be moved by passion for integrity and respect for the intention of the Diaspora to work for the betterment of their home countries.

Leading for Community Building

In extending franchise to the Diaspora, ethical leaders will build community, bringing to memory the rationale utilized by Namibia and South Africa in their very first democratic elections in 1994. These two countries allowed their citizens abroad to vote in the national elections for nation building purposes. Associating the Diaspora in nation building is ever underscored through the act of voting whereby both the leaderships of African and their expatriates agree to work towards a common goal. Working toward a common goal encapsulates the very essence of ethical leadership as the leaders take into account their own purposes and those of the followers in a direction that is beneficial to both of them. In accepting the consensus/compromise leading towards the Diaspora suffrage, the leaders under the "baobab tree" would ensure that no one imposes their will on others, and the goal reached is compatible to all parties involved. As it was in traditional Africa, both the Diaspora and the current leadership would bring their contribution to the table for community/nation building.

Kwame Gyekye (2010) uses Akan proverbs and maxims to make the point on reciprocal obligations in Africa. One of the kind states "The well-being of a man depends on his fellow man" underscoring the fact that a person can count on other members of the community for goodwill, sympathy, compassion, and material support. For African cultures in general, mutual aid stands for a moral obligation. Concretely, when a community member needs support or help to work on his or her farm, the community members is likely to receive such an aid from other members who would expect the same behavior from him or her. African ethics champions altruism or *kimuntu* as a fundamental moral value in a world where one can be overwhelmed by the contingences of daily life. Additionally, traditional African wisdom requires one to share one's roof and food with a stranger. However, three important points need to be made.

First, it appears that traditional African wisdom does not explicitly foster reciprocity across larger communities than the extended family and the ethnicity at best. Second, not clearly decipherable, however, is the obligation for the African leader to enter in a reciprocal relationship with his or her people and share material, psychological, and other social values. One reason might be the traditional leader's divine status which used to set the chief apart from the common people. No wonder some vicious traditional leadership behavior of withholding personal goods and materials from people has been extended nowadays to public assets. Third, in the D.R. Congo for example, many popular sayings illustrate this incapacity not only to share the common goods, but also to care for them and use them for community building (Bongila, 2011).

The leaders under "the baobab tree" would transcend the negative implications of the African culture. The process leading toward the extension of the Diaspora's franchise offers the opportunity to revise traditional divides and impact future generations. This attitude would meet the core character of transformational leadership as Northouse (2010) explains, paraphrasing Burns (1978) as saying that such a leader moves the group in a direction that is beneficial to not only the leader, but particularly the followers. The leaders under "the baobab tree" would take into account both the purposes of the expatriates, those of their citizens back home and their own. They would behave in this way out of sensibility for the interest of the country and those of the cultures involved in the discussion. In agreement with Gilligan's (1982) conception of ethics of care, African leaders would demonstrate a caring ethics toward others by acknowledging each one's intentions. By granting a step-by-step franchise to the expatriates, leaders under "the baobab tree" would acknowledge that the goals of all involved are "bound up in the common good and public interest" (Northouse, p. 393). They would have paid attention to positive ways that changes they have made in the electoral policies would affect the whole community and country. Being ethical leaders, their primary concerns are geared toward the common good of all their citizens on whatever corner of the world they might find themselves residing.

CONCLUSION

This chapter may have helped come to terms with the dilemma that has been lingering throughout the book. The question of whether or not the African Diaspora may hold the right to vote in homeland's elections has come down to a seemingly satisfactory course of action. Indeed, those I have metaphorically referred to as "extended family" ought to vote in the presidential suffrage of their home country as a first step of a full electoral right. Both extreme sides of the protagonists and opponents of the Diaspora's external franchise might rightly feel disappointed with the resolution of this leadership ethics analysis. Why should the Diaspora be reduced to voting only in presidential, and not in the parliamentary and other local elections? Why should one even consider granting such a right to people who live outside their country, and who do not 'face the music' of their votes? These are ethically legitimate questions that convey dissatisfaction with the resolution of the dilemma from both sides. Yet ethicists agree that by its nature a resolution of a dilemma cannot bring full satisfaction to either the lone decision maker or all the parties involved. Ruggiero (2008) underscores the fact that "in a moral dilemma. . . you must choose between two alternatives; there is no third. . . . Look for an indication that one of the two goods is (however slightly) greater than the other or that one of the evils is less evil" (p. 125). In choosing to extend progressively the rights to vote to the Diaspora, I have somehow opted for a higher good and less evil solution, although my position stands slightly between both extremes. In this case, assumption is that African leaders face two evils: granting immediate unconditional election rights to the Diaspora (on the one hand) and denying them any franchise rights (on the other). Therefore, resorting to a progressive franchise can stand for what Aristotle refers to as "middle path." The use of the ethical analysis phase of prudent pragmatism or else "the African baobab tree" allows for a middle-ground-like solution. This middle path can only be achievable when conveners at the "baobab tree," made up of both African leaders and representatives of the Diaspora, abide by the principles of ethical leadership, including respect for each other, service to the community, honesty, justice/fairness, and community building.

Chapter Ten

By Way of Conclusion

The wise continues while the fool is always beginning.
—Zambian Proverb

At the conclusion of this book, it appears suitable to first review some of the thorny points raised by the dilemma of the Diaspora Africans election rights, such as the ethics of external elections, its practicality and implications, as well as the conflict of ethical obligations posed by the pertinence of dual citizenship. In revisiting those questions, I interviewed the former president of Burundi, His Honorable Pierre Buyoya. Twice president of the sub-Saharan country of Burundi (1987–1993 and 1996–2003), Buyoya is member of the respected African Forum (AF), a network for African heads of states and governments, whose purpose is to support the implementation of the broad objectives of the African Union (AU) and its initiatives. The status of former chief of state has given him an honorary appointment as a senator for life in his country. Since 2008, Buyoya has been appointed by the African Union to lead peace missions in such countries as Chad and Sudan, and is still internationally solicited for peacekeeping operations and peace process in various countries including the Central African Republic, Mauritania, and currently in Mali. His most recent book, *Inter Burundian Negotiations: A Long Walk Toward Peace* published in 2011, highly reflects his favorite leadership approach based on the principles of African "baobab tree" I discussed in chapter 9. Although still disputable mainly by those holding an opposite viewpoint to his opinion, Buyoya's position presents a reflection rooted on two solid foundations: on the one hand, his three decades of regional and international public service, on the other hand the reality of the phenomenon of globalization and its multifaceted ramifications, which also affect global leadership ethics. Referring to the underpinning question covered in this book, and the meaning of Diaspora (chapter 1), I put the following question to His Honorable Buyoya: What do you think about the possibility for the African Diaspora to participate in the elections of their home countries? He said:

> The phenomenon of globalization is calling for openness to this question. In Burundi we are past the discussion on whether the Diaspora should vote because our Diasporans do vote in presidential elections. I think both the country of origin and the Diaspora benefit enormously from an open franchise. Note that the concept of Diaspora itself is to change. Twenty five years ago, people considered their Diaspora as a tiny minority, but in this era of globalization, this is no longer true. Take countries like Cape Verde that has most of its population abroad. Those citizens of Cape Verde are and should rightly be in the position to have their own representation in their country's government. Many countries have granted their Diaspora a jurisdictional status; and as such, they can present candidates to elections and elect their own representatives to the country parliament (Buyoya, personal communication, May 25–26, 2013).

Opponents of the Diaspora election rights raised one main objection in relation to duty ethics (chapter 3), utility ethics (chapter 4), and virtues ethics (chapter 5) whereby questioning the feasibility and the economics of expatriate suffrage. My question to Buyoya in this matter goes as follows: How does this work, assuming that a Diaspora is so spread out in various regions and countries of the world. How would the organization of elections be possible? Buyoya argues:

> Diplomatic missions would have to serve as voting places; each embassy or consulate should turn into a voting precinct. This has been the case in Burundi where members of the Diaspora turn to their embassies and diplomatic missions in time of election. The only challenge raised by certain countries is the prohibitive cost of organizing overseas elections, because indeed they cost a lot of money. But whatever that cost, it is important to lend a voice to those vibrant members of the Diaspora; many of them are great contributors to the economies of their home countries. In countries like Nigeria, Cape Verde, and Benin, the Diaspora's dollar contribution in a given year is greater than the sum of foreign aid the country receives. This shows the importance of considering those citizens of Africa living abroad as authentic citizens with full right to their country's elections (Buyoya, personal communication, May 2013).

In citing Burundi as an exemplar in the Diaspora's elections, Buyoya's statement should rectify the IDEA's classification of Burundi among the countries that have "no external voting" (IDEA, 2007, p. 236, and IDEA, 2010) as shown in the appendix's "voting method" of this book. The reader should approach the IDEA's error as an unfortunate oversight that I am unable to correct as it is deemed a direct quote. Chapter 3 of this book also tackles the lingering challenge of dual citizenship and dual loyalty, which many consider to be an ethical impediment to a voting right for the Diaspora. Here is my question to Buyoya: How about the question of dual citizenship and the potential dubious loyalty toward one country, specifically toward the country of origin? His response goes along these lines:

> If the Diaspora was not loyal to their homeland, I hardly understand why they would choose to contribute their remittances? Take well organized Diasporas like those of Benin, Ghana, and Mauritania that contribute enormously to the social development of their homelands, how can this not show real loyalty? The question of dual citizenship or dual loyalty should not be a sufficient reason to prevent valuable members of the Diaspora from exercising their right to vote in homelands. When I was in office, I knew that some of my ministers held two citizenships: They were at once Burundians and French or Belgians and/or Germans. Jokingly, I would jab at them that some of us in the government had less protection than others. And that in case of turmoil in the country, France or Belgium or whatever country whose nationality they held would come to their rescue one way or the other. And this is the case in several countries that have people in the government with various nationalities. The era of globalization allows for a new way of governing that ought to count with the Diaspora, which is well positioned to bring in their countries of origin investors and entrepreneurs; they lobby in favor of their counties, they organize themselves so well as to find better ways to improve the living conditions in their home countries (Buyoya, personal communication, May 2013).

Throughout the book and specifically in chapters 5 and 7, failure by the Diaspora to pay taxes in their countries came across as an infringement to the obligation of citizenship (according to duty ethics), a privation of the greatest good for the greatest number (according to utility ethics), and a lack of compassion for their compatriots (according to virtue ethics). To the question of "In Zimbabwe, President Robert Mugabe has supposedly demanded that the Diaspora pays taxes in exchange for their right to vote; how about the question of paying taxes to home countries?," former president Buyoya had the following to say:

> I don't understand why this would be a requirement for voting in homeland elections. . . . I don't even think this should be a requirement at all. The right to vote does not have to do with the duty to pay taxes to home countries. We don't require that in Burundi, and I am not sure this would be the case in a foreseeable future. I am not sure I would go that far, although each country should regulate according to its own needs and contexts. I am not here speaking for every country in Africa, rather according to our policies and electoral laws in Burundi and my own personal experience of public affairs (Buyoya, personal communication, May 2013).

The above overview of some salient questions that are particularly attribut-
able to the phenomenon of globalization leads me to the twofold aim of this
leadership ethics analysis of the expatriates' vote entitlement in their countries of origin. The first purpose stems from a scholarly move to solve a
global dilemma within the area of ethical leadership, whereby determining
the importance of this leadership trend in decision making. My second goal,
which was prompted by the first one to which it is connected, was to try out
an ethical decision making process (with the acronym DIRR) that Enomoto
and Kramer have proposed in their book *Leading through the Quagmire*,
which I have found to be quite original and so appropriate for my students'
assignments of professional nature at the University of St. Thomas, MN. The
sample dilemma to be analyzed in this case is concerned with whether people
who have left their countries of origin to reside abroad ought to vote in their
African homelands. I have been intent on presenting the DIRR (Description,
Interpretation, Rehearsal, and Re-discernment) model of ethical analysis to
its full extent, not just as it is laid out in Enomoto and Kramer's (2007) book
or a short-term assignment paper, but as an applied strategy for ethical leadership decision making. One unintended purpose calls to mind Foucault's
study of seemingly meaningless topics such as "power" through the evolution of the prison system in *Discipline and Punish* (1977) or the evolution of
the idea of "insanity" in *History of Madness* (1961). Similarly, it might
appear just as not appealing—at first—to engage in a rigorous scholarly
examination of African Diaspora's franchise; yet I have been attracted to
shed some light on an unpopular but fascinating dilemma. I conclude the
resolution of the dilemma by conceding some kind of progressive franchise
to the African Diaspora as a consequence of the analytical tool I utilized. I
shall then look ahead to make a plea for the continuous use and improvement
of an ethical model that adapts well to cases of professional and global
leadership.

LOOKING BACK

What took us to the "baobab tree" though the DIRR model and the process of
prudent pragmatism is an intricate question that can only be addressed when
a deliberative democracy has been adopted as an idealistic political system in
a given nation. Bratton & Mattes (2001) conducted a research on the level of
support for democracy in Africa by assessing the attitude of African citizens
in Ghana, Zambia, and South Africa. Their finding revealed that Africans
value democracy intrinsically, that is as an end in itself. For them "democracy looks better in theory than in practice" (p. 8). There was, however, a high
level of discontent toward instrumental democracy, as a means to improving
material living standards. While Africans are as enthusiastic about democra-

cy as any other Third Wave democratic country, they remain skeptical on its economic and social performance. People's approval hinges more on the government's ability to guarantee basic political rights than its capacity at delivering economic goods. In spite of this rather optimistic view of political rights in Africa, these authors called for the importance of political goods in nation building. While the research reveals that Africans are more optimistic about the political side of democracy, the voting aspect as pertaining to the Diaspora appears much like what Foucault (1977) refers to as "subjugated knowledge," an untouched area of academic research. I realized that ethical leadership can pertinently contribute to the analysis of the Diaspora's suffrage as a democratic process of nation building.

Chander (2001) in his article "Diaspora Bonds" highlights the apparent absence of the African Diaspora in the international arena. He maintains however the central role this body plays in dispatching information about their homelands. Out of their *kimuntu* (African generosity and communitarianism), the Diaspora transmits capital and transforms culture. They defy national borders by challenging the current conception of the nation-state system. As members of one or multiple overseas citizenries and as citizens of their motherlands, their very polyvalent status has eluded scholars until recently. No wonder their request for rights to elections in their birth countries as well as that for dual citizenship falls on deaf ears in most instances. Obviously the option to include the Diaspora into a certain degree of suffrage does not preclude or resolve the lingering question of dual citizenship, which has been allowed in so many countries in the world. This book has conceptualized Diasporas as a topic of ethical leadership inquiry. Whereas Chander tackles legally the issue of multiple citizenships for the Diaspora by proposing some sort of "universal status" for the expatriates, I have preoccupied myself with the morality of elections as a basic component of deliberative democracy. I agree with Chander that a relationship of affinity, which he calls "Diaspora Bonds," some sort of umbilical cord still exists between those members of the Diaspora and their homeland. These "Diaspora Bonds," Chander argues, allow homeland governments to turn to their Diasporas to raise capital for economic development.

Chapter 1 has discussed three categories of the Diaspora: first, those that were uprooted from the motherland through the dehumanizing practice of slavery trade, then there is the first-generation Diaspora, and finally the 1.5 generation in addition to the second and ongoing generations. I have used the metaphor of "extended family" to refer to all of them in spite of the discrepancies in their particular attachment with home countries. To remain within the scope of this ethical leadership study, I have avoided determining the specific categories of Diaspora members that should qualify for franchise. Rather this analysis of the Diaspora involves anyone living overseas whose homeland acknowledges as its own. For example, as various countries have engaged in talks regarding extending citizenship to African-Americans whose DNA tests have linked them to their lands of origin in Africa, this analysis includes their cause. How about political exiles or refugees who find themselves at odds with their home countries' leadership? Or, how about expatriates holding the citizenship of their country of residence while their homelands, such as Zimbabwe, the D.R. Congo, and others, prohibit multiple citizenships? This book has acknowledged them also as members of the "extended family," although the particularities of their statuses necessitate a different undertaking, such as that initiated by Chander (2001) or Sood (2012).

This leadership ethics endeavor began with an intellectual spark caused by the BBC's survey addressing the rights of the Diaspora to the franchise of their home countries. The ethical reformulation of both horns of the dilemma stated in the BBC's survey may come down to whether or not the African Diaspora should vote in their home countries. Coincidently, the BBC has not been alone in this quest, though still in its earliest stage. The first chapter of the book has described the width of the dilemma as well as the individuals and organizations that might be indirectly or directly implicated in the quandary. Most concerned by the dilemma are political leaders of African countries, their home population, and of course their citizens residing outside the country. Questioning and reflection on this matter also came from various scholars. Newland (2010) alludes to voting rights as a way to increase the Diaspora's advocacy. Nesbitt (2003) advocates for a paradigm shift from the Diaspora as brain drain to one that is brain gain. Veney (2002) makes the argument that the African American Diaspora retains linkages to Africa in spite of the social, political, and economic contexts they found themselves in as a result of slavery and its legacy. Mohan (2008) addresses the fine line the leadership of Ghana needs to draw between the economic and political roles, including franchise, its Diaspora can get involved with.

However, those scholars of African Diaspora hardly tackle with exclusivity the dilemma of overseas franchise. Exceptionally, the writings of the Administration and Cost of Elections (ACE) project and those of the International Institute for Democracy and Electoral Assistance (IDEA) have made an invaluable contribution to the subject. The ACE explicitly states that the constitutions of many countries guarantee that all their citizens living outside their national boundaries bear the right to vote. However, the ACE notes, expatriate voters are often disenfranchised given the absence of procedures to enable them to exercise that right. Yet, "Universal—that is, unrestricted and unconditional—external voting is regarded by many as part of the citizen's rights in a world where living or staying abroad forms part of the life of millions of people and where the exercise of rights and the enforcement of laws are becoming more transnational every day" (ACE, 2010b).

With the world ever interconnected at the macro and micro levels, the global and ethical leader is likely to face dilemma questions related to elections in the leader's homeland of the increasing African Diaspora. In order to carefully tackle this dilemma, I chose Enomoto & Kramer's DIRR (Description, Interpretation, Rehearsal, and Re-discernment) methodology of ethical decision making. The presumed thoroughness of this ethical methodology, particularly the uniqueness of its re-discernment phase, helps the global leader to deconstruct and reconstruct the dilemma in a manner that clarifies the most probable course of action to take.

However, I added prudent pragmatism (Bluhm & Heineman, 2007), the "African baobab tree" as a more hands-on phase of the end process during which the conveners effectively work on the deciding moment of the decision making. At first, the DIRR model appears to be tedious and eventually time consuming and unnatural because it is naturally easier to rush to a decision that might be equally ethical as a course of action that follows the proposed analysis. Most scholars of ethical leadership covered in this book advise to the contrary. It is critically important to get used to gathering the necessary information, deconstructing the details gathered, thinking about extraneous elements, and reconstructing those particles in order to shed more light on the challenge in question, and have the satisfaction of making a wiser decision.

This model has the merit to be multidisciplinary. In the current case, I borrowed from political sciences where the question of elections belongs (Brand, 2010); the dilemma also touched international public policy (Chander, 2001), international economy (Velasquez, 2002), international development (Galtung, 1971), sociology and anthropology (Bujo, 2011), educational administration (Shapiro & Stefkovich, 2011), international leadership (Bongila, 2011), and of course ethics, leadership, and leadership ethics (Starratt, 2004). Of most importance is deemed the ability of this model to analyze not only local or national quagmires, but particularly issues of global interests involving social welfare and democracy. Immigration experts and scholars agree on the universal and outgrowing character of the Diaspora. What makes this phenomenon exponentially unfolding are the following examples: the boundaries between nations get more and more porous (Habermas, 2001), the space and time are getting compressed (Harvey, 1990) by the incredible speed of communication and transportation technologies, and more people find it as easy to move to whatever country more attractive jobs take them. Still there is much to the ubiquitousness of the African Diaspora as the first chapter has shown. The description of the African Diaspora reveals a complex issue of the affinity to a native country that should allow one to claim social and political rights. In the interpretation of whether or not the African Diaspora holds the right to vote in their home countries, the global leader might consider kaleidoscopic views balancing ethical challenges and tensions between deontology and utilitarianism and other views in between. This reasoning exercise has helped to "rehearse" four main actions: no action or else not granting the Diaspora any suffrage right at all; granting the African Diaspora full right to external elections; guaranteeing some restricted voting rights to the expatriates; and implementing a step-by-step mechanism for voting abroad. In "re-discerning" the question of external voting, un-tackled relevant issues and other countries' practices were considered that should further enlighten decision making. Using prudent pragmatism, which I referred to as "African baobab tree," the global leader would come to the resolution that the question of the Diaspora suffrage is best solved when the African leadership of each country and its Diaspora sit together to work out suitable mechanisms for external voting. Additionally, structuring those elec-tions might also be subject to debate and consensus in the public sphere. However given the political unwillingness of many African governments to tackle this issue, it is incumbent upon the Diaspora of each country to unite their views in this matter and reclaim the ethical right to elect the leaders of their home country. For the "baobab tree" to be a fruitful exercise of deliber-ative democracy, convening leaders from both sides of the homeland and the Diaspora should gird up the principles of ethical leadership described in Northouse's (2010) *Leadership: Theory and Practice*. These principles in-clude respect of each other's view, service to others, manifestation of hones-ty, use of justice and fairness, and community building. Figure 10.1 sum-marizes the major underpinnings of this book from the discipline of leader-ship ethics to the dilemma of the Diaspora right to franchise.

LOOKING AHEAD

I hope this book has made the point that leadership ethics can bring a special and overdue contribution to global issues with a special emphasis on the Global South. The case of African Diaspora elections represents only one out of gazillion dilemmas that leadership ethics can tackle by means of an en-hanced DIRR method of ethical analysis. My assumption is that sooner or later some issues that have barely been approached in this book, including whether bearers of multiple citizenships ought to vote in their home coun-tries, or whether the rights to vote should require the duty to pay taxes in homelands, will be subjected to an ethical analysis process similar to what was used in this book. These are only a few examples of tough issues for which ethical leaders must use authority in order to mobilize people capable of facing them. Quoting Heifetz, Northouse (2010) agrees that the ethical leader "provides a 'holding environment' in which there is trust, nurturance, and empathy. In a supportive context, followers can feel safe to confront hard problems" (p. 383). I foresee a lasting impact of ethical leadership in Global

Figure 10.1.

South countries and elsewhere whose leaders are intent on bringing about positive and durable change in their nations and organizations. In the same token, this breed of leaders would use authority to direct the attention of the followers, including the Diaspora or other constituents, toward specific issues. They would prompt the followers to act as a reality test regarding information; they would lead them to manage and frame issues; they would encourage them to orchestrate conflicting perspectives; they would finally help them to facilitate decision making. Ethical leadership stands firm as a lasting and timely approach whereby the leader dutifully assists the follower in adopting and adapting with change while embracing personal growth.

One of the modest contributions of this book has been a full blown application of the DIRR model to a case of global importance. Credit should be given to Enomoto and Kramer (2007) for formulating in a more applicable way previous methods of ethical decision making. The task in their hands was to present the model in a compelling manner that did not leave room for its full extent application, though both authors provided illustrations for leaders in educational leadership professions. Mine has been to apply and adapt the method to my most favorite academic and professional endeavor consisting of bridging global and cultural divides of understanding by means of such tool as leadership ethics. Besides topics that are directly related to the ethical leadership and international leadership, other academic areas can also find inspiration from the multidisciplinary ramifications and adaptations this method suggests. For example in a class assignment where students were required to use the DIRR method, two professionals in Educational Leadership stated:

> Although it's done in a much more simplistic manner and we may not even realize we're doing it, I believe these are the things most of us do when we're trying to solve issues. However, this class has provided me with a deep understanding of DIRR method and going forward I will be more intentional with how it's utilized when I make decisions (Ed.S Student, Lakeville, MN).

> I find that knowing and practicing the process of DIRR, "Discernment, Investigation, Rehearsal and Rediscernment," very valuable. As mentioned before, working through this process has helped me to better understand different points of view, how to better evaluate potential solutions to a dilemma, and how to best decide on an ultimate course of action (Ed.S Student, Lakeville, MN).

These statements from professionals other than those in the field of international leadership and ethical leadership indicate that DIRR coupled with prudent pragmatism (African baobab tree) is likely to impact practitioners in several disciplines. While the use and application of "baobab tree" as a method of problem solving might sound familiar to some readers, namely members of African Diaspora and African sociologists and sociologists, it pays to display this process to global leaders for two mere reasons. First, the understanding of the African traditional process of conflict resolution and the democratic principles that are engrained in it, allows for the reader to acknowledge that "African baobab tree" exemplifies major ethical leadership dimensions of nowadays. Talking about the systems of governments that solved their issues under the tree, Ayittey (1998) maintains that "A careful study of [African] societies reveals an astonishing degree of functionality: participatory forms of democracy, rule of customary law, and accountability. Their system of government was so open that some allowed participation by foreign merchants. No modern country, even the United States, can boast of such an open government. Africa's traditional rulers were not despots" (p. 15). The traditional "baobab tree," that I have compared to the process of prudent pragmatism, has encompassed in its own way the principles of ethical leadership analyzed in this book, and this fact needs emphasis. Second, it follows that many conflicts and misunderstanding can be avoided if global leaders, particularly those in Africa that deal with political and civil unrests, would re-discover the mechanisms of meetings under the "baobab tree." It might be understood that I have attempted to revitalize this traditional value for the use of ethical leaders, in particular those in Africa, when analyzing the dilemma of the Diaspora rights to homeland elections. The question beyond the scope of this ethical analysis might come down to what kind of election is most suitable for each country. On the one hand there are no clearly established international or African standards in favor of one electoral system over another. On the other hand, such institutions as the International Institute for Democracy and Electoral Assistance (IDEA) offer a considerable body of literature and comparative studies suggesting systems that may provide a closer connection between parliament, government, and potential Diaspora voters (AfriMAP, 2009).

Finally, how much future relevance would this book hold in the event that all the thirty countries or so in Africa that do not have a provision for external voting (or do not act on such a provision) decide to implement franchise for their Diasporas? Likely this question does not amount to the level of an ethical dilemma whose resolution would take the whole DIRR process. Up to this point, the resolution of this dilemma has led me to hope for the effectiveness of the suffrage rights for the whole "extended family." Whether African Diaspora ought to participate in the elections of their native homes makes only one case study among others that would be deemed relevant to ethical leadership. Although this case study can be done with, or be replaced by more up-to-date dilemmas, many other quagmires of various natures and disciplines will surface that will require the DIRR analysis coupled with prudent pragmatism and, in some contexts, enriched by meetings under the "baobab tree." I do not foresee a *tabula rasa* of the book similar to the distance philosopher Wittgenstein took from his major philosophical work after finding flaws years later (Hacker, 1998). The lingering impact of ethical leadership, the lasting contribution of the DIRR as well as the presumed importance of the "baobab tree" will hopefully continue to inspire students and scholars of various disciplines imbued with the eagerness to contribute to the common good.

References

ACE (2010a). Legal Framework of Voting from Abroad. Retrieved from: http://aceproject.org/ace-en/topics/va/legal-framework?toc See International Convention on the Protection of the Rights of All Migrant Workers and Members of Their Families, UN document A/RES/45/158, December 18, 1990, article 41.

ACE (2010b). Voting from Abroad. Retrieved from: http://aceproject.org/ace-en/topics/va/onePage. The Administration and Cost of Elections (ACE) Project was established in 1998 by IDEA, IFES, and UNDESA. The project was designed to offer a range of services related to electoral knowledge, assistance, and capacity development. The ACE website is a major source of comprehensive information and customized advice on electoral processes.

African Economic Outlook (2012). *Remittances.* Retrieved from: http://www.africaneconomicoutlook.org/en/outlook/financial_flows/remittances/.

AfriMAP (2006). *Democracy and Political Participation.* A Discussion Paper. Johannesburg: Colinton House.

AfriMAP (2009). *Mozambique: Democracy and Political Participation.* Johannesburg: Colinton House.

Akukwe, C. (2009). *Africans in the Diaspora: Development Partnerships.* Retrieved from: http://www.worldpress.org/Africa/3354.cfm.

Allafrica.com (2012). *Nigerian Migrants Remitted U.S. $21 billion Home in 2012.* Retrieved from: http://allafrica.com/stories/201302011272.html.

Archer, V. (2008). Dual Citizenship with the African Diaspora: Why and How African States Can Encourage Diasporans to Return Home as Citizens. Paper presented at African Heads of State and Government for Consideration and Policy Adoption for the Leon H. Sullivan Summit VIII, Tanzania, Arusha.

Aristotle (trans. 2007). *Nicomachean Ethics.* Filiquariam Publishing.

Ayittey, G. (1998). *Africa In Chaos.* New York: St. Martin's Press.

Ayittey, G. (2005). *Africa Enchained: The Blueprint for Africa's Future.* New York: Palgrave Macmillan.

Badaracco, J. L., Jr. (2006). *Questions of Character: Illuminating the Heart of Leadership through Literature.* Boston: Harvard Business School.

BBC News (The British Broadcasting Corporation) (2005). *Zimbabwe Expats Lose Vote Battle.* Retrieved from: http://news.bbc.co.uk/2/hi/africa/4360757.stm.

BBC News (2006). Should the Diaspora Vote? Retrieved from: http://news.bbc.co.uk/go/pr/fr/-/2/hi/africa/4709432.stm.

Beauchamp, T. L. & Bowie, N. E. (eds.) (1988). *Ethical Theory and Business.* Englewood Cliffs: Prentice-Hall.

Bessette, J. (1980). Deliberative Democracy: The Majority Principle in Republican Government. In in R. Goldwin and W. A. Schambra (1980) (eds.) *How Democratic is the Constitution?* pp. 102–116. Washington, DC: AEI.

Bluhm, W. and Heineman, R. (2007). *Ethics and Public Policy: Methods and Cases.* Upper Saddle River: Prentice Hall. 39–67.

Bongila, J. P. (2010). Grounding Political Ethics and African Diaspora Rights to Elections. Paper presented at the African Studies Association Conference. San Francisco, CA.

Borg, R. & Gall, M. (1983). *Educational Research: An Introduction.* (4th ed.) New York: Longman.

Bourdieu, P. (1977). *Outline of a Theory of Practice.* Cambridge: Cambridge University Press.

Bourdieu, P. (1984) *Distinction: A Social Critique of the Judgment of Taste.* Cambridge, MA: Harvard University Press.

Brand, L. (2010). "Authoritarian States and Voting From Abroad: North African Experiences." *Comparative Politics.* 43 (1): 81–99.

Bratton M. and Mattes R. (2001). "Support for Democracy in Africa: Intrinsic or Instrumental?" *British Journal of Political Science.* 31 (3): 447–474.

Braun, N. & Gratschew, M. (2007). Introduction. In *IDEA. Voting from Abroad. The International IDEA Handbook.* Stockholm: International IDEA.

Braziel, J. E. & Mannur, A. (2003). *Theorizing Diaspora: A Reader.* Malden, MA: Wiley-Blackwell.

BuaNews (South African Government News Agency) (2009). *More than 16,000 Expats to Vote in General Elections.* Retrieved from: http://oldsanews.gcis.gov.za/news/09/09040610151004.

Bujo, Benezet (2011). *Foundations of an African Ethic: Beyond the Universal Claim of Western Morality.* New York: The Crossroad Publishing Company.

Burns, J. M. (1978). *Leadership.* New York: Harper & Row.

Business Day (2013). *The Merits and Perils of Diaspora Vote.* Retrieved from: http://businessdayonline.com/2010/07/the-merits-and-perils-of-diaspora-vote-1/.

Bynum, G. L. (2011). Kant's Conception of Respect and African American Education Rights. *Education Theory,* 61(1): 17–40.

Chander, A. (2001). "Diaspora Bonds." *New York University Law Review.* 76, pp. 1,005–1,099. Available at SSRN: http://ssrn.com/abstract=275457 or http://dx.doi.org/10.2139/ssrn.275457.

CIA (2012). *The Worldfactbook.* Retrieved from: https://www.cia.gov/library/publications/the-world-factbook/geos/cv.html.

Creswell, J. W. (2012). *Qualitative Inquiry & Research Design: Choosing Among Five Approaches* (3rd ed.) Thousand Oaks, CA: Sage Publications.

Dalla Costa, J. (1998). *The Ethical Imperative: Why Moral Leadership is Good Business.* Reading, MA: Addison-Wesley.

Dewey, J. (1910). *How We Think.* Buffalo: Prometheus.

Dewey, J. (1960). *The Quest for Certainty.* New York: Capricorn Books.

Davies, R. (2007). Reconceptualising the Migration. Development Nexus: Diasporas, Globalization and the Politics of Exclusion. *Third World Quarterly* 28: 59–76.

Davies R. (2010). Development Challenges for a Resurgent Africa Diaspora. *Journal of International Relations.* University of Plymouth, England. 10: 131–144.

Davis, N. (2011). Contemporary Deontology. In P. Singer (ed.) (2011) *A Companion to Ethics.* pp. 205–219. Malden, MA: Blackwell Publishing.

ECAS (European Conference on African Studies). *Voting Beyond Africa: African Migrants' Political Participation in the Electoral Processes of Their Countries of Origin.* Retrieved from: http://www.nomadit.co.uk/ecas/ecas2013/panels.php5?PanelID=2035.

Ehman, Amy Jo and Sullivan, P. (2001). South Africa Appeals to Canada to Stop Recruiting its MDs. *Canadian Medical Association Journal* (CMAJ). 164(3): 387–388.

EISA (The Electoral Institute of Southern Africa) (2003). *From Military Rule to Multiparty Democracy: Political Reforms and Challenges in Lesotho.* Johannesburg: EISA.

EISA (2005). *Elections and Democratization in Malawi: An Uncertain Process.* (EISA Research Report). Johannesburg: EISA.

EISA (2005). *Multiparty Democracy and Elections in Namibia* (EISA Research Report). Johannesburg: EISA.

EISA (Electoral Institute for Sustainable Democracy in Africa). Namibia Presidential and National Assembly Elections: 27 and 28 November 2009. Johannesburg: EISA.

Enomoto, E. & Kramer, B. (2007). *Leading through the Quagmire. Ethical Foundations, Critical Methods, and Practical Applications for School Leadership.* Lanham, MD: Rowman & Littlefield Education.

Equiano, Olaudah (2007). *The Interesting Narrative of the Life of Olaudah Equiano, or Gustavus Vassa, the African Written by Himself.* London: Dodo Press.

Farrington, C. (2009). Putting Good Governance into Practice I. *Progress in Development Studies*, 9(3): 249–255. doi: http:/ 10.1177/146499340800900305.

Fieser, J. (2009). *The Internet Encyclopedia of Philosophy.* Retrieved from: http://www.iep.utm.edu/ethics/.

Fleshman, M. (2010). *Africa Seeks to Tap Its Diaspora.* Retrieved from: http://www.un.org/en/africarenewal/newrels/diaspora-10.html.

Foucault, M. (1961). *History of Madness in the Classical Age.* J. Khalfa & J. Murphy (trans.) London: Routledge.

Foucault, M. (1977) *Discipline and Punish,* Alan Sheridan (trans.) New York: Pantheon.

Fraser, N. (1990). Rethinking the Public Sphere: A Contribution to the Critique of Actually Existing Democracy. *Social Text.* Duke University Press. 25 (26): 56–80.

Freire, P. (1970) *Pedagogy of the Oppressed.* M.B. Ramos (trans.) New York: Seabury Press.

Freire, P. (1998). *Pedagogy of Freedom: Ethics, Democracy, and Civic Courage.* New York: Rowman & Littlefield.

Fried (1978). Cited by Davis, N. (2011). Contemporary Deontology. In P. Singer (ed.) (2011) *A Companion to Ethics.* pp. 205–219. Malden, MA: Blackwell Publishing.

Fullan, M. (2003). *The Moral Imperative of School Leadership.* Thousand Oaks, CA: Corwin Press.

Galtung, J. (1971). A Structural Theory of Imperialism. *Journal of Peace Research*, 8: 81–118.

Ghananation.com (2012). *Ghanaians in Diaspora Plead with Parties to Accept Supreme Court's Verdict.* Retrieved from: http://www.ghananation.com/news/11357-ghanaians-abroad-plead-with-parties-to-accept-sc-verdict.html.

Gilligan, C. (1982). *In a Different Voice: Psychological Theory and Women's Development.* Cambridge: Harvard University.

Gilroy, P. (1993). *The Black Atlantic: Modernity and Double Consciousness.* Cambridge, MA: Harvard University Press.

Gouinlock, J. (1994). *The Moral Writings of John Dewey.* New York: Prometheus Books.

Gyekye, Kwame (2010). African Ethics. In *Stanford Encyclopedia of Philosophy.* Retrieved from: http://plato.stanford.edu/entries/african-ethics/.

Habermas, J. (1991). *The Structural Transformation of the Public Sphere: An Inquiry into a Category of Bourgeois Society.* (Translation Thomas Burger). Cambridge: The MIT Press.

Hacker, P. M. (1998). Wittgenstein's Place in Twentieth Century Philosophy. In *History and Philosophy of Logic*, 18: 109–14.

Harvey, D. (1990). *The Condition of Postmodernity.* Malden, MA: Blackwell.

Heifetz, R. (1998). *Leadership Without Easy Answers.* Cambridge: Harvard University Press.

Hill, T. E, & Boxill, B. (2001). Kant and Race. In B. Boxill (Ed.), *Race and Racism*, pp. 448–472. New York: Oxford University Press.

Holtved, Ole (2010). Ghana. In Evrensel Astrid (Ed.) *Voter Registration in Africa: A Comparative Analysis.* pp. 103–126. Johannesburg, South Africa: EISA.

IDEA (2007). *Voting from Abroad. The International Handbook.* Stockholm: International IDEA.

IDEA (2010). *Voting Abroad Database.* http://www.idea.int/elections/vfa_search.cfm#.

Ingram, D. & Parks, J. (2002). *The Complete Idiot's Guide to Understanding Ethics.* Indianapolis: Alpha.

International Foundation for the Electoral System (IFES) (2012). *Elections in Angola August 31 Presidential and National Assembly Elections. Frequently Asked Questions.* Washington, DC: http://www.ifes.org/.

Johnson, G.E. (2005). *Meeting the Ethical Challenges of Leadership* (2nd ed.). Thousand Oaks: Sage Publication.

Johnson, G.E. (2011). *Meeting the Ethical Challenges of Leadership* (4th ed.). Thousand Oaks: Sage Publication.

Jones-Correa, M. (2001). Under Two Flags: Dual Nationality in Latin America and its Consequences for Naturalization in the United States. *International Migration Review.* 35: 997–1029.

Judith, A. (2002). *Bioethics as Practice.* Chapel Hill: University of North Carolina Press.

Kant, I. (1960). *Observations on the Feeling of the Beautiful and Sublime.* Trans. John T. Goldthwait. Berkeley: University of California Press.

Kant, I. (1997). *Foundations of the Metaphysics of Morals.* Trans. Lewis White Beck. Upper Saddle River, NJ: Prentice Hall.

Karimi, F. (2011). *Vote Gives 'Lost Boys' Hope for Country's Future.* Retrieved from: http://www.cnn.com/2011/US/01/11/lost.boys.voting/index.html?hpt=C1

Katongele, E. (2011). *The Sacrifice of Africa: A Political Theology.* Grand Rapids: Eerdman Publishing Company.

Kidder, R. (1995). *How Good People Make Tough Choices: Resolving the Dilemma of Ethical Living.* New York: William Morrow & Company.

Kitchener, K. S. (1984). Intuition, Critical Evaluation and Ethics Principles: The Foundation for Ethical Decisions in Counseling Psychology. *Counseling Psychologist,* 12: 43–55.

Kwaku Kyem, P. (2005). The Diaspora Vote: What God Has Given Let No Man Take Away. *Modern Ghana News.* Retrieved from: http://www.modernghana.com/print/117902/1/thediaspora-vote-what-god-has-given-let-no-man-ta.html.

Kwasi, B. E. (2006). Can Second Class Citizens in the Diaspora Beyond Remittances Vote? http://www.ghanaweb.com/GhanaHomePage/NewsArchive/artikel.php?ID=98652#.

Laurence, T. (2005). Moral Equality and Natural Inferiority. *Social Theory and Practice* 31(3): pp. 379–404

Lopez, C. & Theisohn, T. (2003). *Ownership, Leadership and Transformation: Can We Do Better for Capacity Development?* New York: United Nations.

Maame Ama, Djaba (2009). Dual Citizenship: The Benefits of Dual Citizenship to the Socio-economic and Political Development of Ghana. Retrieved from: http://www.ghanadot.com/reviews.djaba.dualcitizenship.090908.html.

Machiavelli, N. (2008). *The Prince.* Trans. Peter Bondanella. New York: Oxford University Press.

MacIntyre, A. (1966). *A Short History of Ethics.* New York: MacMillan.

Magaisa, A. (2009). Citizen Tax: A Flawed Idea. In *New Zimbabwe.* Retrieved from: http://www.newzimbabwe.com/columns-1502'Citizenship+Tax'+a+flawed+idea/columns.aspx.

Manby, B. (2009). *Citizenship Law in Africa: A Comparative Study.* New York: Open Society Institute.

Manning, P. (2009). *The African Diaspora: A History Through Culture.* New York: Columbia University Press. See also I. Okpewho, C.B. Davies, and A. Mazrui (Eds.) (2001). *The African Diaspora: African Origins and New World Identities.* Bloomington: Indiana University.

Marshall, C., & Rossman, G. B. (2006). *Designing qualitative research.* Thousand Oaks, CA: Sage.

Matibe, P. (2009). For Sale: Zimbabwean Diaspora Citizenship and Voting Rights. *Zimbabwe Telegraph,* December 23.

Mbiti, S. J. (1992). *African Religions and Philosophy.* Oxford: Heinemann Educational Publisher.

Mbiti, S. J. (1999). *African Religions and Philosophy* (2nd. ed.). Johannesburg, South Africa: Heinemann Educational Publisher.

Mbola, B. (2009). South Africans Abroad Win Right to Vote. Retrieved from: http://www.southafrica.info/abroad/expats-voting.htm.

Mercer, C., Page, B. & Evans, M. (2008). *Development and the African Diaspora: Place and the Politics of Home.* New York: Zed Books.

Merriam, S.B. (2009). *Qualitative Research: A Guide to Design and Implementation*. San Francisco, CA: Jossey Bass.

Mills, E. J., Kanters, S., Hagopian, A., Bansback, N., Nachega, J., Alberton, M., Au-Yeung, C. G., Mtambo, A., Bourgeault, I., Luboga, S., Hogg, R. S., & Ford, N. (2011). The Financial Cost of Doctors Emigrating from Sub-Saharan Africa: Human Capital Analysis. *British Medical Journal* (BMJ). Online Publication: Published online November 24. doi: 10.1136/bmj.d7031.

Mohan G. (2008). Making Neoliberal States of Development: The Ghanaian Diaspora and the Politics of Homelands. *Environment and Planning: Society and Space*, 26 (3): 464–479.

Morgan, A. Peach, L. and Mazzucelli, C. (Ed.) (2004). *Ethics and Global Politics: The Active Learning Sourcebook*. Bloomfield: Golden Cypress.

Nash, K. (2010). *Contemporary Political Sociology: Globalization, Politics and Power* (2nd ed.) Malden, MA: Wiley-Blackwell.

National Weekly (2007). *Should the Diaspora vote or not?* Retrieved from: http://www.cnweeklynews.com/commentary/editorial/275-should-the-diaspora-vote-or-not.

Navarro, C., Morales, N. & Gratschew, I. (2007). External Voting: A Comparative Overview. In *IDEA, Voting from Abroad. The International IDEA Handbook*. Stockholm: International IDEA.

Nesbitt, FN. (2003). Rethinking Transnationalism: African Intellectuals and the Politics of the African Diaspora. Retrieved from: http://scnc.ukzn.ac.za/doc/AAmwebsite/AAMCONFpapers/Nesbitt,FrancisPaper.doc.

Newland, K. (2010). Voice After Exit: Diaspora Advocacy. *Diasporas & Development Policy Project*. Washington, DC: Migration Policy Institute.

Ninitelamio, Simon-Pierre (2007). Mozambique: A System that is Too Subjective? In IDEA (2007). *Voting from Abroad. The International IDEA Handbook*. Stockholm: International IDEA, pp. 59–65.

Nnaemeka, Obioma (2007). Re-imagining the Diaspora: History, Responsibility and Commitment in an Age of Globalization. *Dialectical Anthropology* 31, 127–141.

Northouse, G. P. (2010). *Leadership: Theory and Practice*. Thousand Oaks: Sage Publication.

Nzeshi, O. (2011). *Nigeria: INEC Proposes Electronic Voting in 2015*. Retrieved from: http://allafrica.com/stories/201111030748.html.

Okpewho, I., Mazrui, A. & Davies, C. (1999).(Eds.). *The African Diaspora: African Origins and New World Identities*. Bloomington: Indiana University Press.

Okpewho, I. & Nzegwu, N. (2003). (Eds.). *The New African Diaspora*. Bloomington: Indiana University Press.

Okpewho, I. & Nzegwu, N. (2009). (Eds.). *The New African Diaspora*. Bloomington: Indiana University Press.

Oxford English Dictionary (OED) (2011). See "Generation." Retrieved from: http://public.oed.com/?post_type=page&s=%22+immigrant+first+generation%22.

Palmer, C. (1998). Defining and Studying the Modern African Diaspora, Quoted in *Perspectives*. Retrieved from: http://www.historians.org/perspectives/issues/1998/9809/9809VIE2.CFM.

Palmer, C. (2000). The African Diaspora. *Black Scholar*, 30(3–4): 56–59.

Pojman, L.P. & Fieser, J. (2012). *Ethics. Discovering right and wrong* (7th ed.). Boston: Wadsworth Centage Learning.

Power, T. J. (2006). Compulsory for Whom? Mandatory Voting and Electoral Participation in Brazil, 1986–2006. Journal of Politics in Latin America. 97–122.

Queye, S. (2011). Ghanaians in the Diaspora Also Want to Vote in 2012. Retrieved from http://news.shaftfmonline.com/2011/11/22/ghanaians-in-diaspora-also-wants-to-vote-in-2012-election/.

Ratha, D. & Xu, Z. (2008). Migration and Remittances. *Factbook 2008*. Washington: The World Bank.

Rawls, J. (1971). *A Theory of Justice*. Cambridge, MA: Harvard University Press.

[Re]brand Africa (2010). *African Citizenship for African-Americans*. Retrieved from http://www.rebrandafrica.org/.

Ruggiero, V. R. (2007). *Thinking Critically About Ethical Issues* (7th. Ed.). Boston McGraw Hill.

Ruggiero, V. R. (2008). *Thinking Critically About Ethical Issues* (7th Ed.). Boston: McGraw Hill.

Shain, Y. & Wittes, T.C. (2002). Peace as a Three-Level Game: The Role of Diasporas in Conflict Resolution. In T. Ambrosio (Ed.), *Ethnic Identity Groups and U.S. Foreign Policy*, pp. 169–199. Greenwood: Praeger Publishers.

Shapiro, J.P. & Stefkovich, J.A. (2011). *Ethical Leadership and Decision Making in Education: Applying Theoretical Perspectives to Complex Dilemmas.* (3rd. ed.) Mahwah: Lawrence Erlbaum.

Shaw, Angus (2011). Nearly One-Third of Zimbabwe's Registered Voters are Dead. Associated Press. Retrieved from http://hanan-revue.blogspot.com/2011/01/group-third-of-zimbabwe-registered.html.

Sood, Suemedha (2012). The Equation of Dual Citizenship. In BBC Travel Tips. Retrieved from http://www.bbc.com/travel/blog/20121004-the-equation-of-dual-citizenship.

SouthAfrica.Info (2009). Retrieved from http://www.southafrica.info/about/democracy/expat-060409.htm.

TheSouthAfrica.com (2012). Voting From Abroad in the 2014 South African Elections. Retrieved from http://www.thesouthafrican.com/news/voting-from-abroad-in-the-2014-south-african-elections-3.htm.

Spring, J. (2009). *Globalization of Education.* New York: Routledge.

Starratt, E. (2004). *Ethical Leadership.* San Francisco: Jossey-Bass.

Staton, J.K., Jackson, R.A. & Canache, D. (2007). Dual Nationality Among Latinos: What Are the Implications for Political Connectedness? *Journal of Politics*, 69(2): 470–482.

Strike, K. & Soltis, J. (2009). *The Ethics of Teaching* (5th ed.). New York: Teachers College Press.

Stuart, H. (Ed.). (1978). *Public and Private Morality.* New York: Cambridge University Press.

Tarimo, A. (2008). *Politicization of Ethnic Identities and the Common Good in Kenya.* Retrieved from: http://www.scu.edu/ethics/practicing/focusareas/global_ethics/kenya.htm.

Thompson, D. (1987). *Political Ethics and Public Office.* Cambridge: Harvard University Press.

Tinga, M. (2010). *African Citizenship for African-Americans.* Posted on [Re]brand Africa (2010). Retrieved from http://rebrandafrica.blogspot.com/2010/07/african-citizenship-for-african.html.

Tungwarara, O. (2007). Zimbabwe: Highly Restrictive Provisions. In IDEA (2007). *Voting From Abroad. The International Handbook.* Stockholm: International IDEA, pp. 56–63.

Tutu, M. D. (2000). *No Future Without Forgiveness.* New York: Doubleday.

UN (2009). Department of Economic and Social Affairs Population Division: *World Population Prospects, Table A.1. 2008 revision.* United Nations. Retrieved from: http://www.un.org/esa/population/publications/wpp2008/wpp2008_text_tables.pdf.

United States Census Bureau (2010). *The Foreign Born Population in the United States: 2010. American community survey reports.* Retrieved from http://www.census.gov/prod/2012pubs/acs-19.pdf.

United States Census Bureau (2012). Nation's Foreign-born Population Nears 37 million. Press Release. Retrieved from http://www.census.gov/newsroom/releases/archives/foreignborn_population/cb10-159.html.

Velasquez, M. (2002). *Business Ethics: Concepts and Cases* (5th ed.). Englewood Cliffs, NJ: Prentice Hall.

Veney R. C. (2002). The Ties that Bind: The Historic African Diaspora and Africa. *African Studies Association, African Issues*, 30, (1): 3–8. Retrieved from: http://www.jstor.org/stable/1167082.

Vengroff, R. (2007). Senegal: A Significant External Electorate. In IDEA (2007). *Voting from Abroad. The International IDEA Handbook*, pp. 104–107. Stockholm: International IDEA.

Watanabe, T. (2009). Called Back to Africa by DNA. More African Americans are Seeking Dual Citizenship and Reconnecting with their Ancestral Homelands thanks to Increasingly

Sophisticated Technology. In *Los Angeles Times*. Retrieved from http://articles.latimes.com/2009/feb/18/local/me-africa18.

Weber, M. (2008). *Protestant Ethics and the Spirit of Capitalism*. New York: BN Publishing.

Webster New Collegiate Dictionary (1974). Springfield, MA: G & C Merriam Co.

The World Bank Group (2010). World Bank Officials Engage African Diaspora in Development Efforts. Retrieved from: http://go.worldbank.org/VL2MO5CIN0.

The World Bank (2011). World Development Indicators 2011 Database and Publication Available now. Retrieved from: http://data.worldbank.org/news/WDI-2011-database-and-publication-available.

The World Bank (2012). African Economic Outlook 2012. Retrieved from http://dx.doi.org/10.1787/888932600165.

Appendix

Table 10.1.   Voting Method

Country	ISO	Voting method
Algeria	DZ	# Personal# Proxy
Angola	AO	Personal (no Diaspora vote in 2013)
Benin	BJ	# Personal# Proxy
Botswana	BW	Personal
Burkina Faso	BF	No external voting
Burundi	BI	No external voting
Cameroon	CM	No external voting
Cape Verde	CV	Personal
Central African Republic	CF	Personal
Chad	TD	# Personal# Proxy
Comoros	KM	No external voting
Congo, Democratic Republic of	CD	In transition
Côte d'Ivoire	CI	Personal
Djibouti	DJ	Personal
Egypt	EG	No external voting
Equatorial Guinea	GQ	Personal
Eritrea	ER	In transition
Ethiopia	ET	No external voting
Gabon	GA	# Personal# Proxy

163

Gambia	GM	No external voting
Ghana	GH	Personal
Guinea	GN	# Personal# Proxy
Guinea-Bissau	GW	Personal
Kenya	KE	No external voting
Lesotho	LS	Postal
Liberia	LR	No external voting
Libyan Arab Jamahiriya	LY	No provisions for direct elections
Madagascar	MG	No external voting
Malawi	MW	No external voting
Mali	ML	# Personal# Proxy
Mauritania	MR	No external voting
Mauritius	MU	Proxy
Mayotte	YT	
Morocco	MA	No external voting
Mozambique	MZ	Personal
Namibia	NA	Personal
Niger	NE	Personal
Nigeria	NG	No external voting
Republic of the Congo (Brazzaville)	CG	No external voting
Reunion	RE	
Rwanda	RW	Personal
Saint Helena	SH	No external voting
Sao Tome and Principe	ST	Personal
Senegal	SN	Personal
Seychelles	SC	No external voting
Sierra Leone	SL	No external voting
Somalia	SO	In transition
South Africa	ZA	Personal
South Sudan	SS	
Sudan	SD	Personal
Swaziland	SZ	No external voting
Tanzania, United Republic of	TZ	No external voting
Togo	TG	Proxy
Tunisia	TN	Personal
Uganda	UG	No external voting

Western Sahara	EH	
Zambia	ZM	No external voting
Zimbabwe	ZW	Postal

Source: IDEA (2010). *Voting Abroad Database*. http://www.idea.int/elections/ vfa_search.cfm#

Index

About the Author

Dr. Jean-Pierre Bongila, EdD, is associate professor of leadership, policy, and administration in the College of Education, Leadership and Counseling (CELC) at the University of St. Thomas (UST), MN. He is the founding and current director of the International Leadership Program at the same institution. Dr. Bongila won the 2002 Council for the Advancement and Support of Education's (CASE) award for the most outstanding dissertation in communication for educational advancement. He is the recipient of the 2011 UST Global Citizenship Award.